MOBY DICK

AN ADAPTED CLASSIC

MOBY DICK

HERMAN MELVILLE

GLOBE BOOK COMPANY
A Division of Simon & Schuster
Englewood Cliffs, New Jersey

Glenn Holder
formerly Head of the English Department
Richmond Senior High School
Richmond, Indiana

Erwin H. Schubert
formerly Head of the English Department
West Milwaukee High School
Milwaukee, Wisconsin

M. Jerry Weiss
Distinguished Service Professor of Communication
Jersey City State College
Jersey City, New Jersey

Cover design: Marek Antoniak
Cover illustration: Paul Biniasz

ISBN: 0-83590-225-0

Printed in the United States of America.
10   9   8

Globe Book Company
A Division of Simon & Schuster
Englewood Cliffs, New Jersey

ABOUT THE AUTHOR

Herman Melville was born in New York in August, 1819. His parents died while he was still very young. Although he attended high school for only a short time, Melville became an outstanding scholar and writer.

Melville tried farming, went to sea, joined the American Navy, taught school, and went on a whaling voyage into the Pacific. It was on this whaling voyage that he collected much of the material he later included in *Moby Dick*. Melville wrote *Moby Dick* in 1851 while he and his family were living in Massachusetts.

After he became well-known for his writing, Melville became a lecturer. He spoke about his visits to Hawaii and the South Sea islands. He was later appointed customs inspector in New York City. After his appointment, Melville continued to write, especially poetry.

Herman Melville died in New York in 1891. Among his most famous books are: *Typee, Omoo, Mardi, Redburn, White-Jacket, Moby Dick, Pierre, The Confidence Man,* and *Billy Budd.*

PREFACE

Moby Dick is a story of the great whaling years in the first half of the nineteenth century. At that time, whale oil was in great demand. City streets were lit with the oil. Many homes and public buildings were lit with gas made from the oil. And, as you will read, American ships dominated the industry. In 1846, over 700 American ships were engaged in whaling.

Since that time, whale oil has lost its importance. Streets and buildings are lit by electricity. Petroleum products have taken the place of whale oil. But whales are still hunted. Many countries now limit or prohibit the capture of certain whales. And modern methods have taken away some of the thrill, daring, skill, and danger that made whaling so exciting.

Moby Dick is an exciting adventure story. It is also the complex story of one man's search for revenge. The battle between a cunning white whale and the man who seeks to kill him is more than it seems. It is the struggle of a man against himself.

ADAPTER'S NOTE

In preparing this edition of *Moby Dick,* Herman Melville's main purpose has been kept in mind. Since the book was originally published, however, language has changed. We have modified or omitted some passages and some vocabulary. We have, however, kept as much of the original as possible.

CONTENTS

SHIPPING TERMS

After hold	The back, lower part of the ship.
Boom	A large timber fastened to the bottom of a sail.
Bow	The forward part of a boat or ship.
Bulwarks	The sides of a ship which extend above the upper deck.
Capstan	A drum used for raising or lowering heavy weights.
Gunwales	The lengthwise strip covering the upper end of the framing timbers in a boat.
Keel	The central structural part in the bottom of a ship.
Loggerhead	A round piece of timber around which the line is turned to keep it from going out too fast.
Maintop	The top of the first sail of the middle mast.
Masthead	A lookout high above the deck of the ship.
Quarter-deck	Afterpost of the ship's upper deck.
Scuttle	An opening in the deck of a ship.
Stern	The rear end of a ship.
Tiller	A lever which turns the rudder.
Windlass	A hoisting machine.

1 *I Start to Sea Again*

Call me Ishmael. Some years ago, having little money in my purse and nothing to interest me on shore, I thought I would sail about a little and see the watery part of the world. Whenever I find myself growing grim about the mouth, pausing before coffin warehouses, and bringing up the rear of every funeral I meet, then I know it is high time for me to get to sea as soon as I can. There is nothing surprising about this feeling since all men have nearly the same feeling toward the ocean.

As certain forces attract the needles of the compasses, so all men, all boys are drawn to the sea, at some time or other. Inlanders, too, from lanes and alleys, streets and avenues—north, east, south, and west—yield to the call of rivers, ponds, lakes, and oceans. Why did the old Persians worship the sea? Surely all this is not without meaning. I only know that I was tormented to sail the seas again, to see things far away and strange.

I do not mean that I go to sea as a passenger. For, to go as a passenger you need to have a purse, and a purse is but a rag unless you have something in it. Besides, passengers get seasick, don't sleep at night, and do not enjoy themselves much, as a general thing. No, I never go as a passenger, nor do I ever go as a captain or a cook.

No, when I go to sea, I go as a simple sailor. True, they order me about, and make me jump from place to place like a grasshopper in a May meadow. What if some old hunk of a sea captain orders me to get a broom and sweep down the decks? Well, then, however the old sea captains may order me about, however they may thump and punch me, I have the satisfaction of knowing that it is all right; that everybody else in one way or another is served in the same way.

Again, I always go to sea as a sailor because they make a point of paying me for my trouble, and they never pay passengers a single penny that I ever heard of. On the contrary, passengers themselves must pay. Finally, I go to sea as a sailor because of the wholesome exercise and the pure air of the top deck of the ship.

After having been a merchant sailor, I now decided to go on a whaling voyage. The main reason I wanted to go on a whaling voyage was the great whale himself. Such a huge and mysterious monster roused my curiosity. Also, the wild and distant seas, where the whale lived, made me wish to go on a whaling voyage.

I stuffed a shirt or two into my old carpet bag, tucked it under my arm, and started, finally arriving in New Bedford on a Saturday night in December. Here I was disappointed when I learned that the little boat for Nantucket had already sailed, and that no way of reaching the place could be found until the following Monday.

Now, having a night, a day, and still another night before me in New Bedford, it was necessary that I find a place to eat and sleep. The night was bitingly cold and cheerless, I knew no one in the place, and I had very little money. After having investigated a number of places, I finally came to a place called "The Spouter Inn

—Peter Coffin," and I decided to go inside. Upon entering the place, I found a number of young seamen gathered about a table. Then I called to the landlord and told him I wished a room, but he said his inn was full; every bed was taken.

"But," he said, "you hain't no objections to sharing a harpooneer's [1] bed, have ye? I suppose if you are goin'

---

[1] A harpooneer was the man who threw the harpoon, or spear, into the whale.

a-whalin', you'd better get used to that sort of thing." I told him I never liked to sleep two in a bed, that if I should ever do so, it would depend upon who the harpooneer might be, and whether he (the landlord) really had no other place for me, and whether the harpooneer was not dangerous. Why, rather than wander further about a strange town on so bitter a night, I would share the man's bed.

"I thought so. All right; take a seat. Supper'll be ready directly."

At last some four or five of us were summoned to our meal in an adjoining room. It was as cold as Iceland—no fire at all—the landlord said he couldn't afford it. But the food was very good—not only meat and potatoes, but dumplings.

Supper over, the company went back to the barroom, when, knowing not what else to do with myself, I decided to spend the rest of the evening as a looker on.

I noticed that one of the guests held somewhat aloof and did not make as much noise as the rest. This man interested me at once, and I will give a little description of him. He stood a full six feet in height, with broad shoulders and a huge chest. I have seldom seen a man so strong. His voice at once announced that he was a Southerner, and I thought he must be one of those tall mountaineers from the Alleghanian Ridge in Virginia. Finally this man slipped away, and I saw no more of him until he became my comrade on the sea. In a few minutes, however, he was missed by his shipmates, and being, it seems, a huge favorite with them, they raised a cry of "Bulkington! Bulkington! Where's Bulkington?" and darted out of the house in pursuit of him.

No man prefers to sleep two in a bed. In fact, you would rather not sleep with your own brother. I don't know how it is, but people like to be private when they are sleeping. And when it comes to sleeping with an unknown stranger, in a strange inn, in a strange town, and that stranger is a harpooneer, then there are many objections. Nor was there any earthly reason why I as a sailor should sleep two in a bed, more than anybody else; for sailors do not sleep two in a bed at sea. To be sure, they all sleep together in one apartment, but you have your own hammock, and cover yourself with your own blankets, and sleep in your own skin.

The more I thought over this harpooneer, the more I disliked the thought of sleeping with him. It was getting late, and any decent harpooneer ought to be home and going bedwards. Suppose, now, he should tumble in upon me at midnight—how could I tell from what vile hole he had been coming?

"Landlord! I've changed my mind about that harpooneer—I shan't sleep with him. I'll try the bench here."

"Just as you please; I'm sorry I can't spare ye a tablecloth for a mattress. The boards are quite rough."

I now measured the bench, and I found that it was a foot too short, and the other bench in the room was about four inches higher, so there was no placing them together. Cold drafts of air, which filled the room, also further convinced me that the plan would never do at all.

Still, looking around me again, and seeing no possible chance of spending the night unless in some other person's bed, I began to think that, after all, I might be thinking wrongly about the harpooneer. Thinks I, "I'll wait awhile. He must be dropping in before long. I'll have a good look at him then, and perhaps we may become jolly good bedfellows after all—there's no telling."

But though the other boarders kept coming in ones,

twos, and threes, and going to bed, yet no sign of my harpooneer.

"Landlord!" said I, "What sort of a chap is he—does he always keep such late hours?" It was now hard upon twelve o'clock.

"No," he answered, "generally he's an early bird, but tonight he went out a-peddling, you see, and I don't see what keeps him so late, unless maybe he can't sell his head."

"Can't sell his head?—what sort of story is this you are telling me?" I demanded, getting into a rage. "Do you pretend to say, landlord, that this harpooneer is actually engaged this blessed Saturday night in peddling his head around this town?"

"Yes, that's it," said the landlord.

"Landlord," said I, "you and I must understand each other without delay. I come to your house and want a bed. You tell me you can give me only half a bed; that the other half belongs to a certain harpooneer. And about this harpooneer, whom I have not yet seen, you tell me terrifying stories. I now demand of you to speak out and tell me who and what this harpooneer is, and whether I shall be safe to spend the night with him. And in the first place, if that story is true, as you say, about his selling his head, I take it to be good evidence that this harpooneer is mad, and I have no idea of sleeping with a madman."

"Well," said the landlord, catching a long breath. "This here harpooneer I have been tellin' you of has just arrived from the South Seas, where he bought up a lot of embalmed New Zealand heads, and he's sold all of them but one, and that one he's trying to sell tonight, 'cause tomorrow's Sunday, and it would not do to be sellin' human heads about the streets when folks is goin' to churches."

This account cleared up the mystery, and showed that the landlord, after all, had no idea of fooling me. "Depend upon it, landlord, that harpooneer is a dangerous man," I said.

"He pays reg'lar," explained the landlord. "But come, it's getting dreadful late. You won't see him tonight. He's come to anchor somewhere. You had better be getting in bed. Won't ye come?"

I considered the matter a moment, and then upstairs we went, and I was shown into a small room, cold as a clam, and furnished, sure enough, with a bed almost big enough for almost any four harpooneers. "There," said the landlord, placing a candle on a crazy old sea chest; "there, make yourself comfortable now, and good night to ye." I turned around from looking at the bed, but he had disappeared.

I sat down on the side of the bed, and commenced thinking about the head-peddling harpooneer. I took off my jacket and coat, and thought some more. But beginning to feel very cold, half undressed as I was, and remembering what the landlord said about the harpooneer's not coming home at all that night, it being so very late, I jumped out of my trousers and boots, and then blowing out the light, tumbled into bed, and gave myself to the care of heaven.

At last I slid off into a light doze, and had pretty nearly gone to sleep when I heard a heavy footfall in the passage, and saw a glimmer of light come into the room from under the door.

Lord save me, thinks I, that must be the head-peddler. But I lay perfectly still and decided not to say a word until spoken to. Holding a light in one hand and the New Zealand head in the other, the stranger entered the room, and without looking towards the bed, placed his candle a good way off from me on the floor in one corner, and then began working away at the knotted cords of a large bag. I was all eagerness to see his face, but he kept it turned aside for some time while he was unlacing the bag's mouth. This done, he turned around, and, good heavens! what a sight! Yes, it's just as I thought. He's a terrible bedfellow. He's been in a fight, got dreadfully cut, and here he is, just from the surgeon. But just then he turned his face to the light, and I saw that it was not cuts but tatoos.

But the harpooneer never noticed me at all. After some difficulty in opening his bag, he commenced fumbling in it and presently pulled out a sort of tomahawk, and a sealskin pocketbook with the hair on. Placing these on an old chest in the middle of the room, he then took out the New Zealand head—a ghastly enough thing—and crammed it down into the bag. Had not the stranger stood between me and the door, I would have bolted out of it.

Even as it was, I thought of slipping out of the window, but it was the second floor back. I am no coward, but I confess I was now as much afraid of him as if it were the devil himself who had thus broken into my room in the dead of night.

Taking up the tomahawk from the table, he examined the head of it for an instant, and then holding it to the light with his mouth at the handle, he puffed out great clouds of tobacco smoke. The next moment the light was extinguished, and this wild cannibal, tomahawk between his teeth, sprang into bed with me. I sang out, I could not help it now; and giving a sudden grunt of astonishment, he began to touch me.

Stammering out something, I knew not what, I rolled away from him against the wall and then begged him, whoever or whatever he might be, to keep quiet and let me get up and light the lamp again. "Who-e debel you?" he said at last. "You no speak-e, I kill-e." And so saying he began to swing the lighted tomahawk about me in the dark.

"Landlord, for God's sake, Peter Coffin!" shouted I. "Landlord! Watch! Save me!"

"Speak-e! tell-ee me who-ee be, or I kill-e," again growled the cannibal, while the swinging of the tomahawk scattered the hot ashes about me until I thought my linen would get on fire. But thank heaven, at that moment the landlord came into the room, light in hand; and leaping from the bed, I ran to him.

"Don't be afraid now," said he, grinning. "Queequeg here wouldn't harm a hair o' your head."

"Stop your grinning," shouted I, "and why didn't you tell me that harpooneer was a cannibal?"

"I thought ye know'd it;—didn't I tell ye he was a peddlin' heads around town? Go to sleep. Queequeg, look here—you sabbee me—this man sleepe you—you sabbee?"

"Me sabbee plenty," grunted Queequeg, puffing away at his pipe and sitting up in bed.

I looked at him for a moment. For all his tattooings he was on the whole a clean-looking cannibal. What's all this fuss I have been making about, thought I to myself—the man's a human being just as I am. He has just as much reason to fear me as I have to be afraid of him.

"Landlord," said I, "tell him to put out his tomahawk there, or pipe, or whatever you call it; tell him to stop smoking, and I will turn in with him. But I don't fancy having a man smoking in bed with me. It's dangerous. Besides, I ain't insured."

This being told to Queequeg, he at once complied, and again politely motioned me to get into bed—rolling over to one side as much as to say—"I won't touch a leg of ye."

"Goodnight, landlord," said I; "you may go."

I turned in, and never slept better in my life.

2 *I See More of Queequeg*

Upon waking next morning about daylight, I found Queequeg's arm thrown about me, which gave me a strange feeling, as you can imagine. When I was a child, I well remember a somewhat similar circumstance that happened to me, and whether it was a reality or a dream, I never could entirely decide. The circumstance was this. I had been cutting up some caper or other—I think it was trying to crawl up the chimney —and my stepmother, who was all the time whipping me or sending me to bed supperless, dragged me by the legs out of the chimney and packed me off to bed. She did this even though it was only two o'clock in the afternoon of June twenty-first, the longest day in the year. I felt dreadful. But nothing could be done, so upstairs I went to my little room on the third floor, undressed myself as slowly as possible so as to kill time, and with a bitter sigh got between the sheets.

Sixteen hours in bed! The small of my back ached to think of it. For several hours I lay there awake, feeling a great deal worse than I have ever felt since. At last I must have fallen into a troubled nightmare of a doze, and slowly waking from it, half in a dream, I opened my eyes and the once sunlit room was now wrapped in outer darkness. Instantly I felt a shock running through all my frame; nothing was to be seen or heard, but a huge hand seemed placed in mine. For what seemed ages piled on ages, I lay there, frozen with the most awful fears, not daring to drag my hand away, yet ever thinking that if I could but stir one single inch, the horrid spell would be broken. I can't remember how I ever escaped from the hand; but on awaking in the morning, I shudderingly remembered it all. And to this very hour I often puzzle myself with it.

If you take away the awful fear of the hand in the nightmare, my feelings were very much alike, in their strangeness, to those which I experienced on waking up and seeing Queequeg's arm thrown about me. But finally all the past night's events came back to me. Even though I tried to move his arm and unlock his clasp, he still hugged me tightly. I then tried to rouse him by calling out, "Queequeg!" but his only answer was a snore. I then rolled over, my neck feeling as if it were in a horse collar, and suddenly I felt a slight scratch. Throwing aside the coverlet, I saw the tomahawk sleeping by the savage's side, as if it were a hatchet-faced baby.

A pretty pickle, truly, thought I. Here I was abed in a strange house with a cannibal and a tomahawk. "Queequeg!—in the name of goodness, Queequeg, wake." At length, after much wriggling and shouting, I succeeded in getting a grunt, and finally he drew back his arm and shook himself all over like a Newfoundland dog just from the water. He then sat up in bed, looked at me and rubbed his eyes as if he did not altogether remember how I came to be there. Meanwhile, I lay quietly watching him, not being seriously frightened now. By certain signs and sounds he gave me to understand that, if it pleased me, he would dress first and then leave the whole room to me. Say what you will, it is marvelous how polite these savages are. I pay this particular compliment to Queequeg because he treated me with such consideration while I was guilty of rudeness, staring at him from my bed and watching all his toilet motions. Nevertheless, a man like Queequeg you don't see every day.

He commenced dressing at the top by putting on his beaver hat, a very tall one, and then, still minus his trousers, he hunted up his boots. What under the heavens he did it for, I can not tell, but his next movement was to crush himself, boots in hand and hat on, under the bed. I could hear him pulling on his boots, though by no law that I have ever heard of is any man required to be private when he is putting on his boots. If he had not been a savage, he never would have dreamed of getting under the bed to put them on.

At last he came out from under the bed with his hat very much dented and crushed down over his eyes, and acting as if his boots pinched him. Since there were no curtains to the window, and the house across the street commanded a plain view into the room, I begged him as well as I could to hurry his toilet and to get into his pantaloons as soon as possible. He did as I asked him and then started to wash himself. At that time in the morning any other person would have washed his face, but Queequeg, surprisingly, washed only his chest, arms and hands.

He then put on his waistcoat, and taking up a piece of hard soap on the washstand center table, dipped it into water and commenced lathering his face. I was watching to see where he kept his razor, when lo and behold, he takes the harpoon from the bed corner, slips out the long wooden stock, unsheathes the head, whets it a little on his boot, and walking up to the bit of mirror against the wall, begins a vigorous scraping, or rather harpooning of his cheeks. Afterwards, I wondered less at this operation when I came to know of what fine steel the head of a harpoon is made, and how exceedingly sharp the long straight edges are always kept. The rest of his toilet was soon achieved, and he proudly marched out of the room, wrapped up in his great monkey jacket, and sporting his harpoon like a town marshal's baton.

When I also had dressed and washed, I went down into the barroom and smiled at the grinning landlord very pleasantly. I could not feel angry with him, even though he had played a prank on me in the matter of my bedfellow.

The barroom was now full of the boarders who had been coming in for some time, and I had not had an opportunity to look them all over. They were nearly all whalemen, a brown and brawny company with long beards. You could pretty plainly tell how long each one had been ashore. This young fellow's healthy cheek is like a sun-toasted pear in hue. He cannot have been three days landed from his Indian voyage. The man next to him looks a few shades lighter.

"Grub, ho!" now cried the landlord, flinging open a door, and in we went to breakfast. I was prepared to hear some good stories about whaling, but to my surprise nearly every man was silent. And not only that; they looked embarrassed. Yes, here was a set of sea dogs, many of whom without the slightest bashfulness had boarded great whalers on the high seas, and yet here they sat at a social breakfast table looking as if they had never been out of sight of the Green Mountains. A curious sight—these bashful bears, these timid warrior whalemen.

But as for Queequeg—why, Queequeg sat there

among them—at the head of the table, too, as cool as an icicle. However, his greatest admirer could hardly have justified his bringing his harpoon to breakfast with him and using it to bring the beefsteaks to his plate.

We will not speak of all of Queequeg's peculiarities here; how he refused coffee and hot rolls and applied all his attention to beefsteaks done rare. But when breakfast was over, he withdrew like the rest to the public room, lighted his tomahawk pipe, and was sitting there quietly digesting and smoking with his hat on when I went out for a stroll. I wanted to take a look at New Bedford.

Think not that this famous town has only harpooneers, cannibals, or country dandies. Still New Bedford is a queer place. Had it not been for us whalemen, that tract of land would this day perhaps have been in as howling condition as the coast of Labrador. As it is, parts of her back country are enough to frighten one; they look so bony. The town itself is perhaps the dearest place in which to live in all New England. The streets do not run with milk; nor in springtime do they pave them with fresh eggs. Yet, in spite of this, nowhere in all America will you find more beautiful houses, parks, and gardens.

Go and gaze upon the iron harpoons round yonder lofty mansion, and you will see what made New Bedford. Yes, all these brave houses and flowery gardens came from the Atlantic, Pacific, and Indian oceans. One and all they were harpooned and dragged hither from the bottom of the sea. By this I mean that money made from the sale of the products of the whale had made possible this splendid city.

3 *I Hear Father Mapple's Sermon*

In this same New Bedford there stands a Whaleman's Chapel, and few are the fishermen bound for the Indian or the Pacific Ocean who fail to make a Sunday visit to the spot. I am sure that I did not.

As I was on my way to church, sleet and mist began to fall. Wrapping myself in my shaggy jacket of the cloth called bearskin, I fought my way against the storm. Entering, I found a small scattered congregation of sailors, sailors' wives, and widows. Silence reigned, broken at times only by the shrieks of the storm. The chaplain had not yet arrived; and there these silent islands of men and women sat watching several marble tablets, with black borders, masoned into the wall on either side of the pulpit. One of them ran something like the following:

Sacred

To the Memory

of

JOHN TALBOT

Who, at the age of eighteen, was lost overboard,

Near the Isle of Desolation, off Patagonia,

November 1st, 1836

This Tablet

Is erected to his Memory

By his Sister

Shaking off the sleet from my ice-glazed hat and

jacket, I seated myself near the door, and turning sideways was surprised to see Queequeg near me. He was the only person present who seemed to notice my entrance, because he was the only one who could not read, and the rest were reading the tablets on the wall.

It needs hardly be told with what feelings, on the eve of a Nantucket voyage, I watched those marble tablets, and by the weak light of that darkened sad day read the fate of the whalemen who had gone before me. Yes, Ishmael, the same thing might happen to you. But somehow I grew merry again.

I had not been seated very long when a stockily built man entered. Yes, it was the famous Father Mapple, so called by the whalemen among whom he was a great favorite. He had been a sailor and a harpooneer in his youth, but for many years past had dedicated his life to the ministry. At the time I now write of, Father Mapple was in the hardy winter of a healthy old age. No one having heard his history, could for the first time see Father Mapple without a great deal of interest. When he entered, I noticed that he carried no umbrella, and certainly had not come in his carriage, for his hat ran down with melting sleet, and his great pilot cloth jacket seemed almost to drag to the floor with the weight of the water it had absorbed. However, hat, coat, and overshoes were one by one removed, and hung up in a little space in a nearby corner. Then he quietly approached the pulpit.

Like most old fashioned pulpits, it was a very high one, and the architect, it seemed, had acted upon the hint of Father Mapple and had finished the pulpit without stairs. Instead there was a rope ladder, like those used in mounting a ship from a boat at sea. Halting for an instant at the foot of the ladder, and with both hands

grasping the ropes, Father Mapple cast a look upwards and then mounted the steps as if mounting the maintop of his vessel. I was not prepared to see Father Mapple, after gaining the height, slowly turn round and stooping over the pulpit, deliberately drag up the ladder step by step until the whole was deposited within.

But the side ladder was not the only strange feature of the place. Between the marble cenotaphs [1] on

[1] Monuments for persons buried elsewhere.

either side of the pulpit, the hall which formed its back was adorned with a large painting representing a gallant ship beating against a terrible storm off a coast of black rocks and snowy breakers. But high above the dark-rolling clouds there floated a little isle of sunlight from which beamed forth an angel's face, and this bright face shed a distinct spot of light upon the ship's tossed deck. "Ah, noble ship," the angel seemed to say, "beat on, beat on, thou noble ship, and bear a hardy helm; for lo! the sun is breaking through. The clouds are rolling off."

Father Mapple rose, and in a mild voice, ordered the scattered people to come closer together. There was a low rumbling of heavy sea boots among the benches, and a still slighter shuffling of women's shoes, and all was quiet again, as every eye was on the preacher. He paused a little. Then kneeling in the pulpit's bows, folded his large brown hands across his chest, uplifted his closed eyes, and offered a prayer so deeply religious that he seemed to be kneeling and praying at the bottom of the sea. Then nearly all joined in singing a hymn, which swelled high above the howling of the storm.

A brief pause followed; the preacher slowly turned over the leaves of the Bible, and at last, folding his hand down upon the proper page, said: "Beloved shipmates, clinch the last verse of the first chapter of Jonah—'And God has prepared a great fish to swallow up Jonah.'

"Shipmates, this book, containing only four chapters—four yarns—is one of the smallest strands in the mighty cable of the Scriptures. Yet what depths of the soul does Jonah's deep sea line sound! But what is the lesson that the Book of Jonah teaches? Shipmates, it is a two-part lesson; a lesson to us all as sinful men, and a lesson to me as a pilot of the living God. As sinful men, it is a lesson to us all because it is a story of the sin, hard-heartedness, suddenly-awakened fears, the swift punishment, repentance, prayers and finally the delivery and joy of Jonah. As with all sinners among men, Jonah had disobeyed the command of God—never mind now what the command was—which he found a hard command. But all things that God would have us do are hard for us to do—remember that—and hence, He oftener commands us than tries to persuade. And if we obey God, we must disobey ourselves.

"With this sin of disobedience in him, Jonah still further mocks God by seeking to flee from Him. He thinks that a ship made by men will carry him into countries where God does not reign. With slouched hat and guilty eye, hiding from his God, Jonah prowled along the ship docks like a vile burglar hastening to cross the seas. So disordered and self-condemning is his look that had there been policemen in those days, Jonah would have been arrested on suspicion.

"At last, after much dodging, he finds a ship; and as he steps on board to see its captain in the cabin, all the sailors for the moment stop hoisting goods and watch the stranger's evil eye.

" 'Who's there?' cries the captain at his busy desk."

" 'I seek a passage in this ship to Tarshish,' says Jonah. 'How soon sail ye, sir?'

" 'We sail with the next coming tide,' says the captain.

" 'I'll sail with ye,' replied Jonah. 'How much is the passage money?' And Jonah paid the fare, which was three times what was usually charged.

"And now the time of tide has come. The ship casts off her cables and glides to sea. But the sea rebels. It will not bear the wicked burden. A dreadful storm comes on, and the ship is in danger of breaking into several pieces. The captain calls all hands to lighten her, and boxes, bales, and jars are tumbled overboard. Aye, shipmates, Jonah was gone down into the sides of the ship and was fast asleep. But the frightened master comes to him and shrieks in his ear, 'O sleeper, arise!'

"Startled from his sleep, Jonah staggers to his feet and stumbles to the deck. But at that moment he is sprung upon by a huge wave leaping over the sides of the ship. Terrors upon terrors run shouting through his soul, and his guilt is too plainly shown. The sailors mark him. More and more certain grow their suspicions of him, and at last, fully to test the truth, by referring the whole matter of high Heaven, they fall to casting lots to see who caused the tempest to come upon them. And the lots say 'Jonah.'

"Jonah now goes on to make a full confession, and the sailors become more and more fearful, but they still are pitiful. For, when Jonah—not yet begging God for mercy, since he knew too well what he deserved—when wretched Jonah cries out to them to take him and cast him into the sea, for he knew that he was responsible for the great storm, they turn from him and seek by other means to save the ship. But these did no good. The angry gale howls louder, and then, with one hand raised to God, they unwillingly cast Jonah into the sea.

"The instant that Jonah is dropped into the water, a calmness floats out of the east and the sea is still. But almost unnoticed to Jonah, he drops into the mouth of a whale, and the whale closes his ivory teeth like so many white bolts. Then Jonah prayed unto the Lord, out of the fish's belly. But notice his prayer and learn a weighty lesson. For sinful as he is, Jonah does not weep and wail for direct deliverance. He feels that his dreadful punishment is just. He leaves all his deliverance to God. And here, shipmates, is true and faithful sorrow for doing wrong. And pleasing to God was this conduct in Jonah as is shown in the final rescue of him from the sea and the whale. Sin not, but if you do, have sorrow for doing wrong as did Jonah."

While he was speaking these words, the howling of the shrieking storm without seemed to add new power to the preacher, who, when describing Jonah's sea storm, seemed tossed by a storm himself. But again he leaned over towards the people, and bowing his head lowly, he continued:

"Then God spake unto the fish, and then the whale came up towards the warm and pleasant sun and vomited Jonah out upon the dry land. And when the word of the Lord came a second time, Jonah, bruised and beaten, did God's bidding. And what was that, shipmates? It was to preach the truth to the face of falsehood! That was it!"

He said no more, but slowly waving a blessing, covered his face with his hands and remained kneeling until all the people had departed, and he was left alone in the place.

I Make a Bosom Friend

Returning to the Spouter Inn from the Chapel, I found Queequeg there quite alone, he having left the Chapel before I did. He was sitting on a bench before the fire, with his feet on the stone hearth, and with a jackknife was gently whittling away at the nose of his little idol and humming as he did so.

With much interest I sat watching him. Savage though he was, and hideously marred about the face, his expression yet had something in it that was by no means disagreeable. You cannot hide the soul. Through all his unearthly tattooings, I thought I saw the traces of a simple, honest heart, and in his large eyes there seemed to be evidence of a spirit that would dare a thousand devils. There was a certain lofty bearing about the pagan, and his head reminded me of the popular busts of General George Washington.

I noticed that Queequeg said very little or nothing at all to the other seamen at the inn. He seemed to have no desire whatever to enlarge the circle of his acquaintances, something which struck me as very strange. Yet upon second thought there was something grand about it. Here was a man some twenty thousand miles from home, thrown among strange people, and yet he seemed entirely at ease and content with his own companionship.

Wild as Queequeg was, I began to feel drawn toward

him. Then I drew my bench near him and made some friendly signs and hints, doing my best to talk with him meanwhile. At first he noticed me very little, but finally when I told him we were to be bedfellows again, he looked pleased. We then turned over the pages of a book together, and I tried to explain to him the purpose of printing and the meaning of the few pictures that were in it. Soon I proposed a social smoke, and producing his pouch and tomahawk, he quietly offered me a puff. And there we sat exchanging puffs from that wild pipe of his, and keeping it regularly passing between us.

When our smoke was over, he pressed his forehead against mine, said that we were bosom friends, and that he would gladly die for me, if need be.

After supper and another social chat and smoke, we went to our room together. He made me a present of his embalmed head; then he took out his enormous tobacco wallet, and searching under the tobacco, drew out some thirty dollars in silver. Spreading the money on the table and dividing it into two equal parts, he pushed one of them toward me and said it was mine. I told him I couldn't take it, but he silenced me by pouring the dollars into my trouser pockets. I let them stay. He then went about his evening prayers, taking out his idol, while I wondered whether I should join him if asked. How could I, a good Christian, unite with this wild savage in worshipping his piece of wood?

Now, Queequeg is my fellowman. And what do I wish that this Queequeg would do for me? Why, unite with me in my particular Presbyterian form of worship. Then, I must unite with him in his. So I kindled some shavings, helped prop up the innocent little idol, offered him burnt biscuit while Queequeg bowed before him two or three times, and kissed his nose. That done, we went to bed and were at peace with the world. But we did not go to sleep without some little chat.

We had lain in bed, chatting and napping, and we felt like getting up again, though daybreak was yet some way down in the future. With our shaggy jackets drawn about our shoulders, we now passed the tomahawk pipe from one to the other until there slowly grew over us a blue cover of smoke. Whether this cloud of blue smoke rolled the savage away to far distant scenes, I know not, but he now spoke of his native island. Eager to hear his history, I begged him to go on and tell it, and he gladly complied. Though at the time I did not understand all his words, I now, having since become familiar with Queequeg's speech, can present the whole story.

Queequeg was a native of Rokovoko, an island far away to the west and south. It is not down on any map. When he was young, running wild about his native woodlands followed by nibbling goats, Queequeg, even then, had a strong desire to see something more of the Christian world than a whaling vessel or two. His father was a high chief, a king; his uncle a high priest, and on his mother's side he boasted aunts who were the wives of unconquerable warriors. There was excellent blood in his veins.

A ship visited his father's bay one day, and Queequeg sought a passage to Christian lands. But the ship had all the seamen needed and would not permit him to go with them, even though his father tried to persuade the captain to take Queequeg. But Queequeg vowed he would still go. Alone in his canoe, he paddled off to a distant strait,[1] which he knew the ship must pass through when she left the island. On one side was a coral reef; on the other a low tongue of land covered with mangrove thickets that grew out into the water. Hiding his canoe, still afloat, among these thickets, he sat down in the stern, paddle in hand, and when the ship was gliding by, like a flash he darted out. He gained the ship, and with one backward dash of his foot, sank the canoe. Then he climbed up the chains, threw himself at full length upon the deck, grappled a ring-bolt there, and swore not to let it go though hacked in pieces.

The captain threatened to throw him overboard,

---

[1] Narrow body of water between two larger bodies of water.

but Queequeg was the son of a king and budged not. Pleased with Queequeg's courage, the captain at last said that he might make himself at home. But this fine young savage never saw the captain's cabin. They put him down among the sailors and made a whaleman of him.

Queequeg then told me the real reason that he wished to leave the island was to learn from the Christians arts to make his people happier and better than they were. But the practices of whalemen soon convinced him that even Christians could be both miserable and wicked, even more so than all his father's heathens. Arrived at last in Sag Harbor and later at Nantucket and seeing how sailors spent their wages in those places, poor Queequeg gave it up for lost. Thought he, "It's a wicked world, and I'll die a pagan." And yet he lived among these Christians, wore their clothes, and tried to talk their language.

By hints I asked him whether he did not expect to go back and become king, since he might now consider his father dead and gone, he being very old and feeble at last accounts. Queequeg answered no, not yet, and added he was fearful that living among Christians had made him unfit for taking the throne of thirty pagan kings before him. But by and by, he said, he would return as soon as he felt himself baptized again. For the present, however, he would sail about and sow his wild oats in all four oceans. They had made a harpooneer of him, and that whaling iron would be used in place of a king's sceptre now.

I asked him what he had in mind to do now, and he answered that it was to go to sea again as a whale harpooneer. Upon this, I told him it also was my intention to leave on a whaler, and from out of Nantucket, since this was the most promising port for an adventurous whaleman to embark from. He at once decided to accompany me to that same island, ship aboard the same vessel, get into the same watch, the same boat, the same mess, and in short to share everything with me. To all this I joyously agreed. For Queequeg, in addition to being my very good friend, was also an experienced harpooneer, and as such could not fail to be of great usefulness to one like me, who was wholly ignorant of the mysteries of whaling. I was, however, well acquainted with the sea as it is known to merchant seamen.

His story being ended with the pipe's last dying puff, we very soon were sleeping.

5 We Go to Nantucket

Next morning, Monday, after selling the embalmed head to a barber, I paid my own and Queequeg's bill, using, however, Queequeg's money. The grinning landlord, as well as the boarders, seemed amazingly tickled at the sudden friendship which had sprung up between Queequeg and me, especially since I once had been so alarmed at Peter Coffin's stories about Queequeg.

We borrowed a wheelbarrow, and, taking our things, went down to the *Moss*, the little Nantucket packet schooner [1] moored at the wharf. We took turns at wheeling the barrow, and Queequeg now and then stopped to adjust the sheath on his harpoon barbs. I asked him why he carried such a troublesome thing with him ashore, and whether all whaling ships did not have their own harpoons. To this he replied that whaling ships did carry harpoons, but that he had a particular love for his own harpoon because it had been tried in many fights with whales.

Shifting the wheelbarrow from my hand to his, he told me a funny story about the first wheelbarrow he had ever seen. At Sag Harbor the owners of his ship had lent him one to carry his heavy chest to his boarding house. Trying not to seem ignorant about the thing,

---

[1] A ship, usually rather small, for carrying mail, passengers and freight.

Queequeg placed the trunk in the barrow and then shouldered the whole thing and marched up the wharf. "Didn't the people laugh?" I asked.

Then he told me another story. The people of his island of Rokovoko at their wedding feasts place the fragrant water of young coconuts into a large stained gourd like a punch bowl, and this punch bowl always forms the central ornament on the mat where the feast is held. Now a certain grand merchant ship once touched at Rokovoko, and its commander was invited to the wedding feast of Queequeg's sister, a pretty young princess just turned ten. Well, when all the wedding guests were assembled at the bride's cottage, this captain marches in and places himself over against the punch bowl and between the high priest and his Majesty the King, Queequeg's father.

After grace was said—for these people have grace the same as we—the high priest opened the banquet by dipping his holy hands and fingers into the bowl. Seeing himself placed next to the priest and noting the ceremony, the captain then washed his hands in the punch bowl, taking it, I suppose for a huge finger bowl. "Now," said Queequeg, "what you tink now? Didn't our people laugh?"

At last, having paid our way on the schooner and made our luggage safe, we stood on board. Hoisting sail, the schooner glided down the Acushnet River, and on one side New Bedford's streets and ice-covered trees were all glittering in the clear, cold air. Mountains of barrels were piled upon New Bedford's wharves, and side by side the world-wandering whale ships lay silent. From other wharves came a sound of carpenters and other workers who were preparing the ships for new cruises.

Gaining the open water, the breeze becoming

stronger, the little *Moss* tossed the quick foam from her bows. Queequeg and I both enjoyed the scene, and thought of many happy days on the sea. So full of the sea scene were we that we did not notice the glances of the passengers. But when an unmannerly young man began to imitate Queequeg, I thought his end had come. Dropping his harpoon, the savage caught him in his arms, and with great strength, sent him high up into the air. When the fellow landed with a hard bump, Queequeg turned his back upon him, lighted his tomahawk pipe, and passed it to me for a puff.

"Captain! Captain!" yelled the lad, running toward that officer. "Captain! Captain! Here's the devil."

"Hallo, you sir," cried the captain, stalking up to Queequeg, "what in thunder do you mean by that? Don't you know you might have killed the chap?"

"What him say?" said Queequeg as he turned to me.

"He say," said I, "that you came near kill-e that man there," and I pointed to the shivering greenhorn.

"Kill-e," cried Queequeg, twisting his tattooed face. "Ah, him very small fish-e; Queequeg no kill-e so small fish-e; Queequeg kill-e big whale!"

"Look you," roared the captain, "I'll kill-e you, you cannibal, if you try any more of your tricks aboard here, so watch what you do!"

But it so happened that it was time for the captain to mind his own business, for the big boom [2] on the schooner was flying from side to side, having become loosened in the wind. And in the excitement the poor fellow whom Queequeg had handled so roughly was swept overboard. The boom flew from left to right and back again, almost in the ticking of a watch, and every instant seemed to be on the point of snapping into

[2] A large timber fastened to the bottom of a sail.

splinters. Nothing was done and nothing seemed capable of being done.

Then Queequeg dropped to his knees, and crawling under the path of the boom, caught the boom with a rope, tied it quickly and all was safe. The schooner was run into the wind, and then Queequeg, stripped to the waist, made a long dive into the sea. For three minutes he was seen swimming like a dog, throwing his long arms out before him. I looked at the grand and

glorious fellow but saw no one to be saved. The green-horn had gone down.

Queequeg now took an instant's glance around him, and seeming to see just how matters were, dived down and disappeared. A few minutes more and he rose again, one arm still striking out and the other dragging a lifeless form. The boat soon picked them up and the boy was restored. All hands voted Queequeg a great fellow, and the captain begged his pardon. From that hour I stayed close to Queequeg.

Queequeg, not seeming to think he deserved all the honor, asked only for water to wash off the brine. That done, he put on dry clothes, lighted his pipe, and watching those around him, he seemed to be saying to himself, "We cannibals must help these Christians."

Nothing more happened on the trip worth mentioning; so, after a fine run, we arrived safely in Nantucket.

Nantucket! Take out your map and look at it. See what a real corner of the world it occupies, how it stands there away off shore. Look at it—a mere small hill and an elbow of sand, all beach without a background. Some will tell you weeds have to be planted there; they don't grow naturally. In olden times, according to an Indian story, an eagle swooped down upon the New England coast and carried off an infant Indian. The parents saw the child carried out of sight over the wide waters, and followed. After a dangerous trip in their canoes, they discovered the island of Nantucket, and there they found an empty ivory casket containing the poor little Indian's skeleton.

It is no wonder, then, that these Nantucketers, born on a beach, should take to the sea for a livelihood. They first caught crabs, and then, growing bolder, waded out with nets for mackerel. More experienced, they pushed off in boats and captured cod. And at last, with a navy of great ships on the sea, they went after the mighty whale.

It was quite late in the evening when the little *Moss* came snugly to anchor, and Queequeg and I went ashore for supper and bed. The landlord of the Spouter Inn had recommended us to his cousin Hosea Hussey of the Try Pots, who, he said, was the owner of one of the best kept hotels in all Nantucket. He also said his cousin was famous for his chowders. By searching about in the dark and by inquiring, we finally came to the hotel that Peter Coffin had recommended.

Standing on the porch at the inn under a dull red lamp hanging there was a freckled woman with yellow hair and a yellow gown. "Come along, Queequeg," said I. "There's Mrs. Hussey." And so it turned out. Mr. Hussey had been called away, and Mrs. Hussey was in charge of the inn.

When we had made known our desire for a supper and bed, Mrs. Hussey seated us at a table and said, "Clam or cod?"

"A clam for supper? A cold clam? Is that what you mean, Mrs. Hussey?" says I. Seeming to hear nothing but the word *clam,* she hurried to an open door leading to the kitchen and bawled out, "Clam for two."

When the smoking chowder came in, the odor was wonderful. Oh, sweet friends, listen to me! It was made of small juicy clams, scarcely bigger than hazel nuts, mixed with pounded ship biscuit and salted pork cut up into little flakes, the whole being enriched with butter and seasoned with pepper and salt. Since we were decidedly hungry from our voyage, it was a wonderful meal. Then thinking I would try a little experiment, I stepped to the kitchen door and said the word *cod.* In a few minutes another wonderful odor came, but with a different flavor, and a fine cod chowder was placed before us.

Fishiest of all places was the Try Pots, which well deserved its name, for the pots there were always boiling chowders—chowder for breakfast, chowder for dinner, and chowder for supper until you begin to look for fishbones coming through your clothes. The area before the house was paved with clam shells, Mrs. Hussey wore a polished necklace made from the backbones of codfish, and Hosea Hussey had his account books bound in shark skin. There was a fishy flavor in the milk, too, which I could not account for until one morning I saw Hosea's cow feeding on fish scraps.

After we had finished supper, we received a lamp and directions from Mrs. Hussey concerning the nearest way to bed. Queequeg started upstairs, but the lady reached forth her arm and demanded his harpoon, explaining that she allowed no harpoon in her chambers. "Why not?" said I. "Every true whaleman sleeps with his harpoon."

"Because it's dangerous," says she. "Ever since young Stiggs was found dead in my first floor back, with a harpoon in his side, I allow no boarders to take such dangerous weapons to their rooms at night. So, Mr. Queequeg, I will just take this here iron and keep it for you until morning. Clam or cod chowder tomorrow for breakfast, men?"

"Both," says I.

I Choose a Whaling Ship

In bed that night we made our plans for the coming
day. But Queequeg, to my surprise, gave me to understand that he had been consulting Yojo (the name of
his little wooden god), and that Yojo had directed that
I, Ishmael, alone must select the ship on which we
would sail. Queequeg placed great confidence in Yojo's
judgment, although the idol's judgment was not always
right. I did not like the plan at all, because I was depend-
ing on Queequeg, who had had much experience with
ships, to point out the whaler best fitted to carry us. But I
could not get Queequeg to change his mind, and I
agreed to select the ship.

Early next morning, leaving Queequeg shut up with
Yojo in our little bedroom, I went out among the shipping—for it was some sort of Ramadan, or day of
prayer and fasting for Queequeg and Yojo. What it was
I could never find out. Although I tried several times, I
could never learn his ceremonies.

Out among the ships I learned there were three
ships ready for three years' voyages. I looked over two
of them, and finally going on board the third, the
Pequod, decided this was the very ship for us. This ship
was named after a famous tribe of Massachusetts Indians, who are no longer in existence. You never saw
such a rare old craft as the *Pequod*. Her masts had been
cut somewhere on the coast of Japan, and her ancient
decks were worn and wrinkled. Old Captain Peleg, a

retired seaman, and the other owners of the ship, had added many unusual things to the *Pequod*. Her upper deck looked like one continuous jaw, with the long sharp teeth of the sperm whale placed there for fastening pins.

Now when I looked about the quarter-deck for someone in authority, at first I saw no one, but I could not overlook a sort of tent pitched behind the mainmast. Here I found a man who seemed to be in charge.

"Is this the captain of the *Pequod?*" said I, advancing to the door of the tent.

"Supposing it be the captain of the *Pequod,* what do you want of him?" he demanded.

"I was thinking of shipping."

"Thou wast, wast thou? I see thou art no Nantucketer. Ever been in a stove boat?" [1]

"No, sir, I never have."

"Don't know anything at all about whaling?"

"Nothing, sir. But I have no doubt I could learn. I've been on several voyages in the merchant service, and I think that—"

"Merchant service be damned! Do not talk about that to me! I suppose ye feel proud of having served in these merchant ships. But, man, what makes thee want to go a-whaling? It looks a little suspicious, don't it? Hast not been a pirate, hast thou? Did not rob thy last captain? You do not think of murdering the officers when thou gettest to sea?"

I told him I was not guilty of any of these things. The old Quakerish [2] Nantucketer seemed not to trust anyone who could be called a stranger.

---

[1] A ship which has been "stoved in," or otherwise damaged, sometimes by a whale.
[2] The Quakers are a Christian religious group; also known as Friends.

"But what takes thee a-whaling? I want to know that before I think of hiring ye."

"Well, sir, I want to see what whaling is. I want to see the world."

"Want to see what whaling is, eh? Have you seen Captain Ahab?"

"Who is Captain Ahab, sir?"

"Aye, aye, I thought so. Captain Ahab is the captain of this ship."

"I am mistaken, then. I thought I was speaking to the captain himself."

"Thou art speaking to Captain Peleg—that's who ye are speaking to, young man. It is the duty of me and Captain Bildad to see that the *Pequod* is fitted out for the voyage and supplied with all her needs, including crew. We are part owners and agents. But as I was going to say, if thou wantest to know what whaling is, as thou sayest, I can tell you how thee can find out before thou signs up to go. Once you have signed it is too late to back out. Look at Captain Ahab, young man, and thou wilt find that he has only one leg."

"What do you mean, sir? Did he lose it in a fight with a whale?"

"Young man, come nearer to me. The leg was devoured, chewed up by the most fierce whale that ever attacked a ship!"

I was alarmed by what he said, but replied as calmly as I could, "What you say is no doubt true enough, sir."

"Sure ye've been to sea before now?"

"Sir," said I, "I thought I told you I had been on four voyages in the merchant—"

"Stop talking about the merchant marine. Don't aggravate me—I won't have it! But let us understand each other. I have given thee a hint about what whaling is; do ye yet feel that you wish to go on the ship?"

"I do, sir."

"Very good. Now art thou the man to pitch a harpoon down a live whale's throat, and then jump after it? Answer, quick!"

"I am, sir, if that should be absolutely necessary, but I don't think such will be absolutely necessary."

"Good again. Now then thou not only wanted to go a-whaling to find out by experience what whaling is, but ye also want to go in order to see the world? Was not that what ye said? I thought so. Well, then just step forward there and take a peep over the weather bow [3] and then come back to me and tell me what ye see there."

Going forward and glancing over the weather bow, I noticed the ship swinging to her anchor and pointing toward the open ocean. The prospect was very forbidding.

"Well, what's the report?" said Peleg when I came back. "What did ye see?"

"Nothing much," I replied. "Nothing but water; considerable horizon, though, and there's a small storm coming up, I think."

"Well, what dost thou think then of seeing the world? Do ye wish to go around Cape Horn [4] to see any more of it? Can't ye see the world where ye stand?"

I was a little staggered, but go a-whaling I must, and the *Pequod* was as good a ship as any. When I told this to Peleg, he said he would hire me. "And thou mayest as well sign the papers right off. Come along." And so saying, he led the way below deck into the cabin.

---

[3] The forward part of the vessel.

[4] Name of the passage, usually stormy, around the southern tip of South America.

Seated in the cabin was a most uncommon and surprising figure, who turned out to be Captain Bildad, another one of the largest owners of the vessel. People in Nantucket invest their money in whaling vessels the same way other people invest theirs in stocks and bonds.

Now Bildad, I am sorry to say, had the reputation of being a hard old man, and in his sea-going days he was known as a bitter master. They told me in Nantucket, though it certainly seems a curious story, that

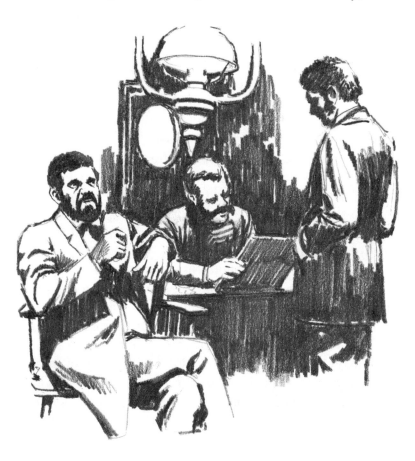

when he sailed the old *Categut* whaleman, his crew, upon arriving home, were mostly all carried ashore to the hospital, exhausted and worn out. He was certainly hard-hearted, to say the least. He never used to swear, though, at his men, but somehow he got a large quantity of hard work out of them. To have Bildad, when he was a chief mate look at you, made you feel completely nervous, and you would clutch something and go to work.

Such then was the person I saw seated when I followed Captain Peleg down into the cabin. Bildad quietly looked up and seeing me, glanced inquiringly toward Peleg.

"He says he's our man, Bildad," said Peleg. "He wants to ship."

"Dost thee?" said Bildad turning around to me.

"I dost," said I.

"What do you think of him, Bildad?" asked Peleg.

"He'll do," said Bildad watching me. I thought him the queerest old Quaker I ever saw, but I said nothing, only looking around me sharply. Peleg now threw open a chest, and drawing forth the ship's articles, placed pen and ink before him and seated himself at a little table. I began to think it was high time to settle with myself at what terms I would be willing to go on the voyage.

I already knew that in the whaling business they paid no wages; but all hands, including the captain, received certain shares of the profits called lays, and the size of the lay a man received depended on the importance of his duties. I was also aware that being a green hand at whaling, my own lay would not be very large. But considering that I was used to the sea, could steer a ship, splice a rope, and all that, I made no doubt from all that I had heard that I should be offered at least the 275th lay—that is, the 275th part of the profit of the voyage. And though the 275th lay was usually not very much, yet it was better than nothing; and if we had a lucky voyage, it might nearly pay for the clothing I would wear out on it, not to speak of my three years' beef and board, for which I would not have to pay a cent.

It might be thought that this was a very poor way to build up a princely fortune—and so it was, a very poor way, indeed. But I am one of those that are never interested in princely fortunes, and am quite content if the world is ready to board and lodge me. Upon the whole, I thought the 275th lay would be about the fair thing, but would not have been surprised if I had been offered the 200th, considering I was of broad-shouldered make.

"Well, Captain Bildad," said Peleg, "what d'ye say, what lay shall we give this young man?"

"Thou knowest best," was the reply. "The 777th wouldn't be too much, would it?"

Such a lay, thought I! The 777th!

"Why, blast your eyes, Bildad," cried Peleg, "thou dost not want to swindle this young man! He must have more than that."

"Seven hundred and seventy-seven," again said Bildad without lifting his eyes.

"I am going to put him down for the 300th," said Peleg. "Do ye hear that, Bildad? The 300th lay, I say."

Bildad laid down the Bible he was reading, and turning solemnly toward him, said, "Captain Peleg, thou hast a generous heart; but thou must consider the duty thou owest to the other owners of this ship—widows and orphans, many of them. If we too abundantly reward this young man, we may be taking the bread from those widows and those orphans. The 777th lay, Captain Peleg." Bildad was clearly angry, and so was Peleg.

Alarmed at this argument between the two main

owners of the ship, I had an idea of giving up sailing in the vessel. I stepped aside from the door to make way for Bildad, who seemed eager to get away from Peleg. But to my surprise, he sat down again very quietly, and seemed not to have the slightest intention of withdrawing. He seemed quite used to Peleg and his ways.

As for Peleg, after letting off his rage as he had, there seemed no more left in him, and he, too, sat down like a lamb.

"Bildad," said Peleg, "thou used to be good at sharpening a lance; mend that pen, will ye? Thank ye, Bildad. Now then, my young man, Ishmael's thy name, didn't ye say? Well then, down ye go here, Ishmael, for the 300th lay."

"Captain Peleg," said I, "I have a friend with me who wants to ship, too. Shall I bring him down tomorrow?"

"To be sure," said Peleg. "Fetch him along, and we'll look at him."

"What lay does he want?" groaned Bildad, glancing up from the book in which he had again been burying himself.

"Oh! never thee mind about that, Bildad," said Peleg. "Has he ever whaled it any?" he asked, turning to me.

"Killed more whales than I can count, Captain Peleg."

"Well, bring him along then."

And, after signing the papers, off I went, not doubting but that I had done a good morning's work and that the *Pequod* was the ship that Yojo had provided to carry Queequeg and me around the Cape.

But I had not proceeded far when I began to think that the captain with whom I was to sail had not yet been seen by me. Of course, it often happened that a whale ship would be completely fitted out and receive all her crew on board before the captain would arrive to take command. For sometimes these voyages are so long and the time at home so exceedingly brief, that if a captain has a family or something else that concerns him, he does not trouble himself much about his ship in port, but leaves her to the owners until all is ready for sea. However, it is best to have a look at the captain before signing yourself away into his hands. Turning back, I met Captain Peleg and asked where Captain Ahab could be found.

"And what dost thou want of Captain Ahab? You already have been hired."

"Yes, but I should like to see him."

"But I don't think thou wilt be able to at present. I don't know exactly what's the matter with him, but he keeps close inside the house. Sort of sick, and yet he don't look so. In fact, he ain't sick; but no, he isn't well either. Anyway, young man, he won't always see me, so I don't suppose he will thee. He's a queer man, Captain Ahab—so some think—but a good one. Oh, thou'lt like him well enough, no fear, no fear. He doesn't speak much, but when he does speak, then you may well listen. Ahab's above the common. He's been in colleges as well as among the cannibals. He's Ahab, boy, and Ahab of old, thou knowest, was a crowned king!"

"And a very vile one. When the wicked king was slain, the dogs, did they not lick his blood?"

"Come here to me," said Peleg, with something in his eye that scared me. "Look ye, lad; never say that on board the *Pequod*. Never say it anywhere. Captain Ahab did not name himself. It was a foolish idea of his crazy widowed mother, who died when he was only twelve months old. I know Captain Ahab well; I sailed with him as mate years ago. I know what he is—a good man—something like me, a swearing good man. I know that he was never very jolly, and I know that on the way home he was out of his mind for awhile, but it was the sharp, shooting pains in his bleeding stump that brought that about, as any one might see. I know, too, that ever since he lost his leg during the last voyage by that whale, he has fits of bad temper sometimes, but that will all pass off. And once for all, let me tell thee and assure thee, young man, it's better to sail with a moody good captain than with a laughing bad one. So good-bye to thee, and wrong not Captain Ahab because he happens to have a wicked name. Besides, my boy, he has a wife, a sweet girl, to whom he had not been wedded very long. Since by that sweet girl that old man has a child, can there be any hopeless harm in Ahab? No, no, my lad."

As I walked away, I was full of thoughtfulness. What had been told me about Ahab made me unhappy about him. And somehow at the time, I felt a sympathy and a sorrow for him, but why I don't know, unless it was the cruel loss of his leg. And yet I also felt a strange awe of him, which was not exactly fear. I do not know what it was. But I felt it, and it did not make me hate him. I felt impatience at what seemed like mystery in him, since I knew so little about him. However, at length my thoughts were carried in other directions, and I forgot Ahab.

7 *I Witness a Ramadan*

As Queequeg's Ramadan, or fasting, was to continue all day, I did not choose to disturb him until toward nightfall, for I have the greatest respect towards everybody's religion. Queequeg had the most unusual notions about Yojo and his Ramadan; but what of that? Queequeg thought he knew what he was doing, and there I let him rest.

Toward evening when I felt his Ramadan must be over, I went up to the room and knocked at the door, but there was no answer. I tried to open it, but it was fastened inside. "Queequeg," said I softly, but all was silent. "I say, Queequeg! Why don't you speak? It's I, Ishmael." But all remained still as before, and I began to grow alarmed. Since it had been such a long time that he had been in the room, I thought he might be sick. I looked through the keyhole, but I could see nothing but part of the bed and wall.

I was surprised to see resting against the wall the wooden shaft of Queequeg's harpoon, which the landlady had taken from him before we had gone to our bedroom. That's strange, thought I; but at any rate, since the harpoon stands yonder and since he seldom goes anywhere without it, he must be inside. "Queequeg! Queequeg!" I shouted again, but all was still. Something must have happened. I tried to open the door, but found I couldn't budge it. Running downstairs, I quickly stated my fears to the first person I met—the chambermaid.

"La! La!" she cried, "I thought something must be

the matter. I went to make the bed after breakfast, and the door was locked. And not a mouse was to be heard, and it has been just so silent ever since. But I thought maybe you had both gone off and locked your baggage for safekeeping. La! La! ma'am—Mistress! Murder! Mrs. Hussey!" And with these cries, she ran toward the kitchen, I following. Mrs. Hussey soon appeared.

"Woodhouse!" cried I. "Which way to it? Run, for God's sake and fetch something to pry open the door. The axe! The axe! He's had a stroke, depend upon it!"

"What's the matter with you, young man?" demanded Mrs. Hussey.

"Get the axe! For God's sake, run for the doctor, someone, while I pry the door open."

"Look here," said the landlady. "Look here. Are you talking about prying open any of my doors?" And with that she seized my arm. "What's the matter with you? What's the matter with you, shipmate?"

In as calm but as rapid a manner as possible, I gave her to understand the whole case. She thought for a moment, and then said, "No, I haven't seen it since I put it there." Running to a little closet under the landing of the stairs, she glanced in, and returning, told me that Queequeg's harpoon was missing.

"He's killed himself," she cried. "God pity his poor mother. Has the poor lad a sister? What's that noise there? You, young man, stop that!" And running up, she caught me as I was again trying to force open the door.

"I won't allow it. I won't have my house spoiled. Go for the locksmith; there's one about a mile from here. But stop!" She put her hand into her side pocket and said, "Here's a key that'll fit, I guess. Let's see." And with that she turned it in the lock. But the door would not come open, because Queequeg had bolted it from the inside.

"Have to burst it open," said I, and was running down the entry a little for a good start when the land-lady again told me not to damage her house. But I tore from her, and with a sudden bodily rush, dashed myself against the door.

With a loud noise, the door flew open, and the knob slamming against the wall sent the plaster to the ceiling. And there, good heavens! there sat Queequeg, alto-gether cool and collected, right in the middle of the room squatting and holding Yojo on the top of his head. He looked neither one way nor the other and had hardly a sign of active life.

"Queequeg," said I, going up to him, "Queequeg, what's the matter with you?"

"He hain't been a-sittin' so all day, has he?" said the landlady.

But not a word could we drag out of Queequeg. I almost felt like pushing him over so as to change his position, since in all probability he had been sitting so for upwards of eight or ten hours, going too without his regular meals.

"Mrs. Hussey," said I, "he's alive at all events; so leave us, if you please, and I will see to this strange affair myself."

Closing the door upon the landlady, I tried to have Queequeg take a chair, but he would not. There he sat. He would not move a peg, nor say a single word, nor even look at me, nor even notice me in any way.

I wonder, thought I, if this can possibly be a part of his Ramadan. Do they fast that way in his native island? It must be so. Yes, it's part of his religion, I suppose. Well, then, let him rest. He'll get up sooner or later, no doubt. It can't last forever, thank God, and his Ramadan comes only once a year.

I went down to supper. After sitting a long time listening to the long stories of some sailors, I went upstairs to bed feeling quite sure by this time Queequeg must certainly have ended his Ramadan. But no; there he was just as I had left him. He had not stirred an inch. I began to grow annoyed with him. It seemed so senseless to be sitting there all day and half the night in a cold room holding a piece of wood on his head.

"For heaven's sake, Queequeg, get up and shake yourself. Get up and have some supper. You'll starve; you'll kill yourself, Queequeg." But not a word did he reply.

Giving up hope, I decided to go to bed and to sleep, and no doubt before a great while he would follow me. But before I turned in, I took my heavy bearskin jacket and threw it over him, as it promised to be a very cold night and he had nothing but his ordinary jacket on.

For some time, do all I would, I could not get into the faintest doze. I had blown out the candle, and the mere thought of Queequeg, not four feet off, sitting there in that uneasy position, alone in the cold and dark, made me very wretched. Think of it, sleeping all night in the room with a wide-awake pagan in this dreary Ramadan!

But somehow I dropped off at last, and knew nothing more until break of day. Looking over the side of the bed, I saw Queequeg squatting as if he had been screwed down to the floor. But as soon as the first glimpse of the sun entered the window, up he got, with stiff joints, but with a cheerful look. He limped toward me where I lay and said his Ramadan was over.

Now, as I have said before, I have no objection to any person's religion, be what it may, so long as that person does not kill or insult any other person because that other person doesn't believe it also. But when a man's religion becomes a torment to him, and makes this earth an uncomfortable place to live in, then I think it high time to take that person aside and argue the point with him.

And that is just what I did with Queequeg. "Queequeg," said I, "get in bed now and listen to me." I then went on to tell him about religions, past and present, but I don't think Queequeg understood me very well or cared, in some cases, for my ideas. Finally, he no doubt thought he knew a good deal more about the true religion than I did.

At last we rose and dressed, and, Queequeg, taking a hearty breakfast of chowders so that the landlady would not make much profit on account of his Ramadan, we started out to board the *Pequod*.

8   *We Meet Elijah, the Prophet*[1]

As we were walking down the end of the wharf towards the ship, Queequeg carrying his harpoon, Captain Peleg shouted that he had not known my friend was a cannibal and that he would not let any cannibals on board unless they had produced their papers.

"What do you mean by that, Captain Peleg?" said I, now jumping on the ship and leaving my comrade standing on the wharf.

"I mean," he replied, "that he must show his papers."

"Yes," said Captain Bildad in his hollow voice. "He must show that he is a Christian church member."

"He is a member of the first Congregational Church," I said.

"What!" cried Bildad. "Deacon Deuteronomy's church? I never saw him going there. Young man, thou art joking with me. What church dost thou mean? Answer me."

"I mean, sir, the same ancient church to which all of us belong; the great first Congregation of this whole worshipping world."

"Young man," said Peleg, "I never heard a better sermon. Why Father Mapple himself couldn't beat it. Come aboard, come aboard; never mind the papers. I say, tell Quohog there—what's that you call him? Tell Quohog to step along. By the great anchor, what a harpoon he's got there. Looks like good stuff, and he han-

---

[1] One who foresees events.

dles it about right. I say, Quohog, or whatever your name is, did you ever stand in the head of a whaleboat? Did you ever strike a fish?"

Without saying a word, Queequeg, in his wild sort of way, jumped upon the bulwarks and from there into the bows of one of the whaleboats hanging to the side, and then bracing his left knee and aiming his harpoon, cried out in some such way as this—

"Cap'ain, you see small drop tar on water dere? You see him? Well, spose him one whale eye, well, den!" And taking sharp aim at it, he darted the iron right over Bildad, across the decks of the ship, and struck the glistening tar spot right in the middle.

"Now," said Queequeg, quietly hauling in the line, "spos-ee him whale-e eye; why dat whale dead."

"Quick, Bildad," said Peleg, his partner, who, afraid of the flying harpoon, had retreated toward the cabin. "Quick, I say, you, Bildad, and get the ship's papers! We must have Hedgehog, there, I mean Quohog, in one of our boats. Look ye, Quohog, we'll give ye the 90th lay, and that's more than ever was given a harpooneer yet out of Nantucket." So down we went into the cabin, and to my great joy Queequeg was soon listed among the same ship's company to which I myself belonged.

When Peleg had everything ready for signing, he turned to me and said, "I guess Quohog there don't know how to write, does he? I say, Quohog, blast ye! Dost thou sign thy name or make thy mark?" Queequeg, who had taken part in signing ship's papers two or three times before, took the offered pen and copied upon the paper, in the proper place, a queer round figure which was tattooed upon his arm.

In the meantime Captain Bildad sat watching Queequeg, and at last Bildad said, "I must do my duty by thee, Queequeg. I am part owner of this ship and feel concerned for the souls of all its crew. I ask thee not to cling to thy pagan ways."

"Stop that, Bildad," said Peleg. "You are spoiling our harpooneer. Religious harpooneers never make good voyagers. It takes the shark out of 'em. No harpooneer is worth a straw who ain't pretty sharkish."

"Peleg! Peleg!" said Bildad, lifting his eyes and hands. "Thou hast seen many a dangerous time; thou knowest what it is to have the fear of death. How can you talk that way? Tell me, when this same *Pequod* here had her three masts overboard in that typhoon off Japan, that same voyage when thou went mate with Captain Ahab, didst thou not think of Death and Judgment then?"

Bildad said no more, but, buttoning up his coat, walked on deck where we followed him. There he stood, very quietly watching some sailmakers who were mending a topsail. Now and then he stopped to pick up a patch or save an end of the tarred twine which otherwise might have been wasted.

"Shipmates, have ye shipped in that ship?"

Queequeg and I had just left the *Pequod*, and were for the moment each occupied with his own thoughts, when the above words were put to us by a stranger, who pointed his finger at the vessel in question. He was shabbily dressed in a faded jacket and patched trousers, and a rag of a black handkerchief was hanging around his neck. Smallpox had disfigured his face.

"Have ye agreed to go in that ship?" he repeated.

"You mean the ship *Pequod*, I suppose," said I, trying to gain a little more time for an uninterrupted look at him.

"Yes, the *Pequod*—that ship there," he said, drawing back his whole arm, and then rapidly shoving it straight out from him, with his finger pointing like a bayonet toward the ship.

"Yes," I said, "we have just signed to go."

"Anything down there about your souls?"

"Queequeg," said I, "let's go. This fellow has broken loose from somewhere. He's talking about something and somebody we don't know."

"Stop!" cried the stranger. "Ye said true—ye haven't seen Old Thunder yet, have ye?"

"Who's Old Thunder?" said I, noting that the stranger was in dead earnest.

"Captain Ahab."

"What! the captain of our ship, the *Pequod*?"

"Yes, among some of us old sailor chaps he goes by that name. Ye haven't seen him yet, have ye?"

"No, we haven't. He's sick, they say, but is getting better, and will be all right again before long."

"All right again before long!" laughed the stranger in a hateful sort of way.

"What do you know about him?"

"What were you told about him? Say that!"

"They didn't tell much of anything about him; only I've heard that he's a good whale hunter, and a good captain to his crew."

"That's true, that's true—yes, both true enough. But you must jump when he gives an order. Step and growl; growl and go—that's the word with Captain Ahab. But were you told nothing about the thing that happened to him off Cape Horn long ago, when he lay like dead for three days and nights? Nothing about that deadly fight with the Spaniard before the altar in Santa? Heard nothing about that? And nothing about losing his leg on the last voyage? Didn't ye hear a word about them matters and something more? No, I don't think ye did; how could ye? Perhaps ye've heard about the leg and how he lost it. Oh yes, almost everyone knows that—I mean they know that he has only one leg and that a whale took the other one off."

"My friend," said I, "what all this chatter of yours is about I don't know, and I don't much care. It seems to me that you must be a little damaged in the head. But if you are speaking of Captain Ahab, of that ship there, the *Pequod*, then let me tell you that I know all about the loss of his leg."

"All about it, eh—sure you do—all?"

"Pretty sure."

With finger pointed and eye leveled at the *Pequod*, the beggar-like stranger stood for a moment, as if in a troubled dream, and said—"Ye've shipped, have ye? Names down on the papers? Well, well, what's signed is signed. And what's to be will be, and then again perhaps it won't be, after all. Anyway, it's all fixed and ready, and some sailors or other must go with him, I suppose. God pity 'em. Morning to ye, shipmates, morning. May the heavens bless ye. I'm sorry I stopped ye."

"Look here, friend," said I, "if you have anything important to tell us, out with it. But if you are only trying to make us afraid, you are not going to be able to do that, that's all I have to say."

"And it's said very well, and I like to hear a chap talk up that way. You and others like you are just the men for him. Morning to ye, shipmates, morning! Oh, when you get on the ship, make it known that I am not going along on the voyage."

"Ah, my dear fellow, you can't fool us that way— you can't fool us. It is the easiest thing in the world for a man to look as if he had a great secret in him."

"Morning to ye, shipmates, morning."

"Morning it is," said I. "Come along, Queequeg, let's leave this crazy man. But stop, tell me your name."

"Elijah."

"Elijah!" thought I, and we walked away, talking about the ragged old sailor and agreeing that he was nothing but a humbug. But we had not gone perhaps a hundred yards when I noticed that Elijah was following us. Somehow, the sight of him struck me so that I said nothing to Queequeg about it, but passed on with my comrade, anxious to see whether the stranger would turn the same corner that we did. He did, and then it seemed to me that he was continuing to follow us, but for what reason I could not understand. Elijah's talk about the *Pequod* and Ahab now came back to me and caused me to wonder.

I decided to find out whether Elijah was really following us, and we turned to retrace our steps. But Elijah passed on without seeming to notice us. This relieved me, and once more I pronounced him in my heart a humbug.

9 We Set Sail

A day or two passed, and there was great activity aboard the *Pequod.* Not only were the old sails being mended, but new sails were coming on board, as were bolts of canvas and coils of rigging. Captain Peleg seldom or never went ashore, but sat on the deck keeping a sharp lookout on the workers. Bildad did all the purchasing and providing at the stores, and the workers kept at their jobs until long after nightfall.

On the day following Queequeg's signing, word was given at all the inns where the ship's company were stopping that their chests must be on board before night, for there was no telling how soon the vessel might be sailing. So Queequeg and I got down our personal belongings, but decided to sleep ashore until the last. But it seems they always give very long notice in these cases, and the ship did not sail for several days. But no wonder, there was a good deal to be done, and there is no telling how many things to be thought of before the *Pequod* was fully equipped.

Everyone knows what a large number of things—beds, saucepans, knives and forks, shovels, tongs, napkins, and what not are necessary to the business of housekeeping. Just so with whaling, which requires a three-years' housekeeping upon the wide ocean, far from all grocers, doctors, bakers, and bankers. And although this also holds true of merchant vessels, yet not by any means to the same extent as with whalemen. For besides the great length of the whaling voyage, the numerous articles necessary to whaling and the impossibility of replacing them at remote harbors, it must be remembered that of all ships, whaling vessels are the most exposed to accidents of all kinds. Thus, provided were the spare boats, spare spars, and spare lines and harpoons, and spare everything, almost, but a spare captain and another ship.

At the period of our arrival at the island, the heaviest supplies for the *Pequod,* which included beef, bread, water, fuel, and iron hoops and staves, had all been placed on board. But, as before hinted, for some time there was a continual fetching and carrying on board of odds and ends, both large and small.

Chief among those who did the fetching and carrying was Captain Bildad's sister, a lean old lady of a most determined and tireless spirit, but very kindhearted, who was determined if she could help it that all the necessary supplies should be aboard the *Pequod* when the ship put out to sea. At one time she would come on board with a jar of pickles for the steward's pantry, and another time with a roll of flannel for the small of someone's rheumatic back. Never did any woman better deserve her name, which was Charity. And like a sister of charity, Aunt Charity would rush about ready to turn her heart and hand to anything that promised to yield safety, comfort, and consolation to all on board a ship in which her beloved brother Bildad was concerned, and in which she herself owned a score or two of well-saved dollars.

As for Bildad, he carried about with him a long list of the articles needed, and at every fresh arrival, down went his mark opposite the article upon the paper. Every once in a while Peleg roared at the men at work.

During these days of preparation, Queequeg and I often visited the ship, and as often asked about Captain Ahab, and how he was, and when he was going to come on board his ship. To these questions they would answer that he was getting better and better, and was expected aboard every day. In the meantime the two captains, Peleg and Bildad, were attending to everything necessary to fit the vessel for the voyage. If I had been downright honest with myself, I would have seen very plainly in my heart that I did not like being signed up under a man whom I had not seen. But I said nothing and tried to think nothing.

At last it was given out that sometime next day the ship would certainly sail. So next morning Queequeg and I were off to an early start.

It was nearly six o'clock, but it was still somewhat dark when we came near the wharf. "There are some sailors running ahead there, if I see right," said I to Queequeg. "It can't be shadows."

"Stop!" cried a voice, whose owner, at the same time coming close behind us, laid a hand upon both our shoulders. It was Elijah. "Going aboard?"

"Hands off, will you!" said I.

"Lookee here," said Queequeg, shaking himself, "go 'way!"

"Ain't going aboard, then?"

"Yes, we are," said I. "But what business is that of yours? Do you know, Mr. Elijah, that I consider you to be out of your place? We are going to the Indian and Pacific oceans, and do not wish to be stopped."

"Ye be, be ye? Coming back before breakfast?"

"He's cracked, Queequeg," said I. "Come on."

"Holloa!" cried Elijah when we were a few paces away from him.

"Never mind him," said I. "Queequeg, come on."

But he stole up to us again, and suddenly clapping his hand upon my shoulder, said, "Did ye see anything looking like men going toward that ship awhile ago?"

Struck by the question, I answered by saying, "Yes, I thought I did see four or five men, but it was too dim to be sure."

"Very dim, very dim," said Elijah. "Morning to ye."

Once more we left him, but once more he came softly after us, and touching my shoulder, he said, "See if you can find 'em now, will ye?"

"Find who?"

"Morning to ye! Morning to ye!" he replied, again moving off. "Oh! I was going to warn ye against—but never mind, never mind. Shan't see ye again very soon, I guess." And with these cracked words he finally left.

At last stepping on board the *Pequod,* we found everything quiet, not a soul moving. Going forward, we found the slide of the scuttle open. Seeing a light, we went down, and found only an old sailor there, wrapped in a tattered pea jacket. In deep slumber, he was thrown at whole length upon two chests, his face downwards and enclosed in his folded arms.

"Those sailors we saw, Queequeg, where can they have gone to?" asked I, looking at the sleeper. But Queequeg had not seen the figures on the wharf. I might have felt myself mistaken about them had not Elijah mentioned them, too. But I didn't say anything further about the matter.

Queequeg removed himself to just beyond the head of the sleeper, and lighted his tomahawk pipe. I sat at the feet, and we kept passing the pipe over the sleeper. The strong smoke, now completely filling the hole, began to tell upon the sleeper. He seemed troubled in the nose, turned over once or twice, and then sat up and rubbed his eyes.

"Holloa!" he breathed at last. "Who be ye smokers?"

"Shipped men," answered I. "When does she sail?"

"Ye are going in her, be ye? She sails today. The captain came aboard last night."

"What captain—Ahab?"

"Who but him indeed?"

I was going to ask him some further questions concerning Ahab when we heard a noise on deck.

"Holloa! Starbuck's around," said the man. "He's a lively chief mate and a good man. I must help him." And so saying he went on deck and we followed.

It was now clear sunrise. Soon the crew came on board in twos and threes, and several of the shore people were busy bringing in various last things on board. But Captain Ahab stayed in his cabin and was not to be seen.

At length toward noon, after the *Pequod* had been hauled out from the wharf, and after the ever-thoughtful Charity had come off in a whale boat, with her last gifts—a nightcap for Stubb, the second mate, and a spare Bible for the steward—after all this, the two captains, Peleg and Bildad, came from the cabin, and turning to the chief mate, Peleg said—

"Now, Mr. Starbuck, are you sure everything is right? Captain Ahab is all ready—just spoke to him— nothing more to be got from the shore, eh? Well, call all hands, then."

As for Captain Ahab, no sign of him was yet to be seen; only they said he was in the cabin. But then the idea was that his presence was by no means necessary in getting the ship off and steering her well out to sea. Indeed, as that was not his proper business, but the pilot's; and, as he was not completely recovered—so they said—therefore Captain Ahab stayed below. All this seemed natural enough; especially as in the merchant marine, many captains never show themselves on deck for a considerable time after heaving up the anchor.

But there was not much chance to think over the matter, for Captain Peleg was now all alive. He seemed to do most of the talking and commanding, and not Bildad.

"Up, everybody," he cried, as the sailors lingered at the mainmast. "Mr. Starbuck, drive up, up!"

"Man the capstan.[2] Jump!"—was the next command, and the crew sprang for the handspikes. I paused on my handspike and told Queequeg to do the same, when I felt a sudden sharp poke. Turning around, I was horrified when I saw Captain Peleg. That was my first kick.

"Is that the way they work in the merchant service?" he roared. "Spring, thou sheep-head. Spring and break thy backbone. Why don't ye spring, I say, all of ye—spring! Quohog! Spring thou chap with the red whiskers; spring there, Scotchcap; spring thou, green pants! Spring, I say, all of ye, and spring your eyes out!" And so saying he moved along the windlass,[3] here and there using his leg very freely.

At last the anchor was up, the sails were set, and off we glided. It was a sharp cold Christmas, and as

---

[2] A drum used for raising or moving heavy weights.
[3] A hoisting machine.

the short northern day became night, we found ourselves upon the broad wintry ocean, whose freezing
spray cased us in ice. The long rows of teeth on the
bulwarks glistened in the moonlight, and like the white
ivory tusks of some huge elephant, vast curving icicles
hung from the bows. In spite of the cold winter night
in the wild Atlantic, in spite of my wet feet and wetter
jacket, there was yet, it then seemed to me, many a
pleasant day to come.

At last we were far enough out into the ocean that
Peleg and Bildad, who had guided the ship from the
port, were no longer needed. The stout sailboat that
had accompanied us began coming alongside. Poor old
Bildad hated to say goodbye. He paced the deck, ran
down in the cabin to speak another farewell, and again
came on deck. Peleg was much calmer, but a tear
showed in his eye when the lantern came close.

But, at last, he turned to his comrade, with a final
sort of look about him,—"Captain Bildad—come, old
shipmate, we must go. Back to the mainyard there.

Stand by to come close alongside, now! Careful, careful! Come, Bildad, boy—say your last. Luck to ye, Starbuck —luck to ye, Mr. Stubb—luck to ye, Mr. Flask—goodbye, and good luck to ye all—and this day three years I'll have a hot supper smoking for ye in old Nantucket. Hurrah and away!"

"God bless ye, and have ye in His Holy keeping, men," murmured old Bildad. "I hope ye'll have fine weather now, so that Captain Ahab may soon be moving among ye—a pleasant sun is all he needs, and ye'll have plenty of them in the tropic voyage ye go. Be careful in the hunt, ye mates. Don't damage the boats needlessly, ye harpooneers. Don't forget your prayers, either."

"Come, come, Captain Bildad, stop talking—away!" And with that, Peleg hurried him over the side, and both dropped into the boat.

Ship and boat separated; the cold, damp night breeze blew between; a screaming gull flew overhead; we gave three heavy-hearted cheers, and blindly plunged into the lone Atlantic.

10 *Something About Whales*

Many are the men, small and great, old and new, landsmen and seamen, who have written of the whale. Run over a few—the Authors of the Bible, Aristotle, Linnaeus, Owen, Scoresby, Beale, Bennett, and others. Of this list of whale authors, some had not seen a whale, but one of them was a real harpooneer and whaleman. I mean Captain Scoresby. On the separate subject of the Greenland or right-whale, he is the best existing authority. But Scoresby knew nothing and says nothing of the great sperm whale, compared with which the Greenland whale is almost not worth mentioning.

And here be it said that the Greenland whale is not the king of the seas, even though some writers have said that he is. He is not even by any means the largest of the whales. Some of the great poets of past days will tell you that the Greenland whale was to them the monarch of the seas. But hear ye! good people, the Greenland whale is no longer king—the great sperm whale now reigneth!

There are only two books in being which at all pretend to put the living sperm whale before you. Those books are Beale's and Bennett's. Both in their time were surgeons to English South Sea whale ships, and both were exact and reliable men. The material touching the sperm whale to be found in their volumes is small, but so far as it goes it is of excellent quality. As yet, however, the sperm whale is not described completely in any literature. His is an unwritten life.

Now the various kinds of whales need some sort of classification, if only an easy outline. As no better man has tried to do this, I shall try myself. I promise nothing complete. It is a ponderous task; no ordinary letter sorter in the postoffice is equal to it. To grope down into the bottom of the sea after them is a fearful thing. But I have swum through libraries and sailed through oceans; I have had to do with whales with my hands; I am in earnest, and I will try.

In his *System of Nature*, 1776, Linnaeus declares, "I hereby separate the whales from the fish" on account of "their warm bilocular [1] heart, their lungs, their movable eyelids, their hollow ears..." I told all this to some friends in Nantucket, both messmates of mine on a certain voyage, and they united in the opinion that the reasons set forth were not sufficient. One of them hinted that the reasons were humbug. I take the good old-fashioned ground that the whale is a fish, and call upon the holy Jonah to back me.

This thing settled, the next point is in what respect does the whale differ from other fish? Above, Linnaeus has given you those items. But in brief, they are these: lungs and warm blood. All other fish are lungless and cold-blooded.

A whale is a spouting fish with a flat horizontal tail. There you have him. A walrus spouts much like a whale, but the walrus is not a fish. Almost anyone must have noticed that all fish familiar to landsmen have not a flat, but a vertical, or up and down tail.

Now, then, we come to the grand divisions of the entire whale host. Whales can be divided into three

---

[1] Having two parts.

main types: the Folio, the Octavo, and the Duodecimo.

The Folios include the sperm whale, the right whale, the finback whale, the humpback whale, the razorback whale, and the sulphur-bottom whale. The sperm whale is without doubt the largest inhabitant of the globe, the most dangerous to capture, and by far the most valuable since he is the only creature from which that valuable substance spermaceti [2] is obtained. Spermaceti was once exceedingly scarce, and it was used not for light but for salves and other medicines. It was only to be had from druggists as you nowadays buy an ounce of rhubarb.

The right whale, the first of the whales hunted by man, yields an article known as whalebone, but the oil from the right whale is not nearly so good as is the oil from the sperm whale. The right whale has for more than two centuries past been hunted by the Dutch and

[2] A waxy solid in the head of the sperm whale.

English in the Arctic seas. It is the whale which the American fishermen have long hunted in the Indian Ocean, on the Brazil Banks, on the Nor' West Coast, and various other parts of the world, all of which spots were called Right Whale Cruising Grounds.

The finback has been seen in almost every sea, and is commonly the whale whose distant jet is seen by passengers crossing the Atlantic from New York. His grand distinguishing feature, the fin, from which he derives his name, is very easily seen. Even if not the slightest other part of the creature be visible, this fin, some three or four feet long with a sharp-pointed end, at times can be seen sticking out above the surface. When the sea is moderately calm, this fin stands up and casts shadows upon the surface, and in so doing it resembles a sundial. The finback does not prefer to travel with other whales. He seems a whale-hater, as some men are man-haters.

Another of the first group is the humpback whale, which is seen on the northern American coast. He has been frequently captured there and towed into harbor. He has a great pack on him like a peddler, but his oil is not very valuable.

Of the little razorback whale not much is known except for his name. I have seen him at a distance off Cape Horn. Though no coward, he has never yet shown any part of himself but his back, which rises in a long, sharp ridge. Let him go—I know little more of him, nor does anybody else.

The last of the first class is the sulphur-bottom whale, who is another retiring gentleman. He is seldom seen. At least I have never seen him except in the far southern seas, and then always at too great a distance to study him. He is never chased. I can say nothing more that is true of him; nor can the oldest Nantucketer.

First of the second group is the grampus whale, who is well known to fishermen, yet he is not classed by them as a whale. However, he is a whale. He varies in size from fifteen to twenty-five feet in length, and he swims in herds. He is never regularly hunted, though his oil is considerable in quantity and pretty good for light.

The black whale of the grampus group averages some sixteen or eighteen feet in length and is found almost everywhere. When not more profitably employed, the sperm whale hunters sometimes capture the black whale to keep up with the supply of cheap oil, for some housekeepers, in the absence of company, sometimes use this tallow instead of the perfume-like wax. Though their blubber [3] is very thin, some of these whales will yield you upwards of thirty gallons of oil.

In the same group is the narwhal or nostril whale, named, I suppose, from his peculiar horn being originally mistaken for a peaked nose. The creature is some sixteen feet in length, while its horn averages five feet, though some exceed ten, and even attain to fifteen feet. What purpose this ivory horn or lance answers would be hard to say. It does not seem to be used like the blade of the swordfish and billfish, though some sailors tell me that the narwhal uses it for a rake in turning over the bottom of the sea for food. One man said the horn was used for an ice-piercer, for the narwhal, rising to the surface of the polar sea and finding it sheeted with ice, thrusts his horn up and so breaks through. But this may not be correct. The oil of the narwhal is very good, clear, and fine, but there is little of it, and he is seldom hunted. He is found mostly in the seas around the polar regions.

Another of the second group is the killer whale, but

[3] The fat of the whale.

very little is known about him. From what I have seen of him at a distance, I should say that he is about the size of the grampus. He is very savage, and he sometimes takes the great folio whales by the lip, and hangs there like a leech until the mighty brute is worried to death. The killer is never hunted, and I have never heard what kind of oil he has.

Last of the second class is the thrasher whale, who is famous for his tail, which he uses in thrashing his foes. Still less is known of the thrasher than of the killer. Both are outlaws, even in the lawless seas.

To those who have not chanced to study the subject, it may seem strange that the third class, the porpoises, which usually do not exceed four or five feet, should be called whales. However, they are whales, since my definition says a whale is a spouting fish with a horizontal tail.

First of this class is the huzza porpoise, which is found almost all over the globe. A well-fed huzza will yield you one gallon of good oil, but the fine delicate fluid from his jaws is exceedingly valuable. It is in request among jewelers and watchmakers. It may never have occurred to you that a porpoise spouts, but the next time you have a chance, watch him. He is really a great sperm whale on a small scale. Porpoise meat is good eating, too.

The algerine porpoise, who is very savage, is found, I think, only in the Pacific. I have fished for him many times, but never yet have seen him captured.

The mealy-mouthed porpoise is the largest of the porpoises, and is found only in the Pacific, so far as it is known. His oil is much like that of the common porpoise.

At the porpoises my whale system ends. However, there may be other whales—I am not certain.

11 *Ahab's Officers*

The chief mate of the *Pequod* was Starbuck, a native of Nantucket and a Quaker. Good-looking and thirty years of age, Starbuck did his work especially well and strongly inclined to superstition. He was definitely not the daredevil type, and his love for his wife and child kept him from taking chances. "I will have no man in my boat," said Starbuck, "who is not afraid of a whale." By this he seemed to mean that the most useful men on a whaler were those who always kept from taking any unnecessary chances and that an utterly fearless man is a far more dangerous comrade than a coward.

"Ay, ay," said Stubb, the second mate, "Starbuck, there, is as careful a man as you'll find anywhere in this fishery."

Starbuck had no fancy for lowering for whales after sundown; nor for fighting a whale that fought back too much. "For," thought Starbuck, "I am here in this ocean to kill whales for my living, and not to be killed by them for theirs." And that hundreds of men had been so killed, Starbuck well knew. Where in the bottomless deeps could he find his own father and brother?

Yet brave as he might be in the face of whales or seas, he was the type of person that might not withstand the terror of an enraged and mighty man. But more about that later.

Stubb was the second mate. He was a native of
Cape Cod; and hence was called a Cape-Cod-man. Happy-
go-lucky, Stubb was neither afraid nor especially brave,
and took dangers as they came without saying much
about it. Good-humored, easy and careless, he presided
over his whale boat as if the most deadly battle were but
a dinner and his crew all invited guests. What he thought
of death itself there is no telling. Whether he ever thought
of it at all might be a question. But if he ever did chance
to cast his mind that way after a comfortable dinner, no

doubt he thought it was something which he would find out when the right time came. Stubb's short, black little pipe was one of the regular features of his face. He kept a whole row of pipes ready loaded, stuck in a rack by his bunk, within easy reach of his hand. Whenever he turned in, he smoked them all out in order. For when Stubb dressed, instead of first putting his legs into his trousers, he put his pipe into his mouth.

The third mate was Flask, a native of Tisbury, in Martha's Vineyard. A short, ruddy young fellow, he had the idea that all whales had injured him personally, and he felt he must destroy as many as possible. He did not at all appreciate the marvel of the wonderful whale, and in his poor opinion a whale was nothing more than a large water rat. He followed whales for the fun of it, and a three years' voyage around Cape Horn was only a jolly joke that lasted that length of time.

Now these three mates—Starbuck, Stubb, and Flask—were important men, for they commanded three of the *Pequod*'s boats as headsmen. In that grand order of battle in which Captain Ahab would collect his forces to move on the whales, these three headsmen were like captains of companies. And since in this famous fishery, each mate or headsman is always accompanied by a harpooneer, it is necessary that in this place we set down who the *Pequod*'s harpooneers were and to what headsman each of them belonged.

First of all was Queequeg, whom Starbuck, the chief mate, had selected for his harpooneer. Stubb's harpooneer was Tashtego, and Flask's harpoon man was Daggoo.

12 _I Meet Ahab_

For several days after leaving Nantucket, nothing was seen of Captain Ahab. The mates, regularly relieving each other at the watches, seemed to be the only commanders of the ship. But they sometimes came from the cabin with sudden orders which made it plain that they themselves were under orders. Yes, their supreme lord was there, though he was not seen by any eyes not permitted to go into the cabin. Every time I went upon the deck from my watches below, I always looked for the captain, because I could not forget Elijah's remarks about him.

But it was the three chief officers of the ship, the mates, who gave me confidence and cheerfulness about the voyage. Three better men, each in his own different way, could not readily be found.

Now, it being Christmas when the ship shot from out her harbor, for a time we had biting weather, though all the time we were running away from it to the southward. We were gradually leaving the merciless winter and all its bad weather behind us. It was one of those gray mornings before we had come upon the good weather, when with a fair wind the ship was rushing through the water, that I mounted to the deck at the call of the forenoon watch. As I looked over the deck, shivers ran over me. There was grim Captain Ahab standing upon his quarter-deck.

There seemed no sign of common bodily illness

about him, nor of the recovery from any. His whole high, broad form seemed made of solid bronze. Threading its way out from among his gray hairs and continuing right down one side of his scorched face and neck until it disappeared in his clothing, you saw a white, slender, rod-like mark. Whether that mark was born with him or whether it was the scar left by some desperate wound, no one could certainly say. The scar was seldom mentioned, especially by the mates.

So powerfully did the whole grim figure of Ahab affect me, that for the first few moments I did not notice that much of his grimness was due to the white leg upon which he partly stood. It had been told me that this ivory leg had been made at sea from the polished bone of the sperm whale's jaw.

Upon each side of the *Pequod*'s quarter-deck there was an auger hole bored about half an inch or so into the plank. His bone leg steadied in that hole, one arm elevated, Captain Ahab stood erect, looking straight out into the sea. There was firmness and wilfulness in his fixed and fearless glance.

Not a word he spoke. Nor did his officers say anything to him, though by their gestures and expressions they showed they were uneasy sailing under Ahab. In a little while, after this first visit in the air, he withdrew into his cabin.

After that morning, he was every day seen by the crew, either standing in his pivot hole or seated upon an ivory stool he had, or heavily walking the deck. As the sky grew less gloomy, we saw him more and more often, as if when the ship had sailed from home, nothing but the bleak winter had kept him out of sight. The warm weather more than once brought forth from Ahab the faint blossom of a look, which, in any other man, would have soon flowered out in a smile.

And by and by it came to pass that he was almost continually in the air. But as yet, for all that he said or did as far as was seen on the sunny deck, he seemed as unnecessary there as another mast. But the *Pequod* was only making a passage now, since she was not in whaling waters, and the mates easily could take care of the ship.

Some days went by, and the *Pequod* at last went rolling through the bright spring of the tropics. For the sleeping man it was hard to choose between wonderful days and wonderful nights.

Old age is always wakeful, and among sea commanders the old graybeards will often leave their berths to visit the night-cloaked deck. It was so with Ahab. Only that now, of late, he seemed so much to live in the open air, that truly speaking, his visits were more to the cabin than from the cabin to the planks. "It feels like going down into one's tomb," he would mutter to himself, "for an old captain like me to be going down this narrow scuttle."

So almost every twenty-four hours, when the watches of night were set, Ahab would come on deck, gripping the iron banister to help his crippled way.

Although Ahab usually was careful not to disturb the men in his nightly walks, Stubb once reminded him there might be some way to stop the noise his ivory limb made on the deck by padding the end of it. Angered at Stubb's suggestion, Ahab shouted back, "Am I a cannon ball, Stubb? But go thy ways. I had forgot. Go below to thy bed. Down, dog, to thy kennel!"

Surprised, Stubb was speechless for a moment, and then said excitedly, "I am not used to be spoken to that way, sir. I do but less than half like it, sir."

"Begone!" gritted Ahab between his set teeth.

"No, sir. Not yet," said Stubb boldly. "I will not tamely be called a dog, sir."

"Then be called ten times a donkey, and a mule, and an ass, but begone, or I'll clear the world of thee!"

As he said this, Ahab moved angrily toward Stubb, who left the scene.

"I was never served so before without giving a hard blow for it," said Stubb as he found himself going down into the cabin scuttle. "It's very queer. I don't know whether to go back and strike him or go down on my knees and pray for him. It's queer, very queer, and he's queer, too. He's about the queerest old man Stubb ever sailed with. How he flashed at me! Is he mad? Anyway, there's something on his mind as sure as there must be something on a deck when it cracks. He ain't in his bed now, either, more than three hours out of the twenty-four, and he don't sleep then. Didn't that Dough-Boy tell me that of a morning that he always finds the old man's hammock clothes all rumpled and tumbled, and the sheets down at the foot? I guess he's got what some folks ashore call a conscience. Well, well, I don't know what it is, but the Lord keep me from catching it. He's full of riddles. I wonder what he goes into the after hold for every night, as Dough-Boy tells me he suspects. What's that for, I should like to know? Who's made appointments with him in the hold? Ain't that queer, now? But didn't he call me a dog? Blazes, he called me ten times a donkey, and piled a lot of jackasses on top of that! He might as well have kicked me and done with it. Maybe he did kick me, and I didn't see it, I was so frightened by his angry face. What the devil's the matter with me? I don't stand right on my legs. Coming up against the old man has sort of turned me wrong side out."

When Stubb had departed, Ahab stood for a while leaning over the bulwarks. And then, as had been usual with him of late, calling a sailor of the watch, he sent him below for his ivory stool and his pipe. Lighting the pipe and planting the stool on the weather side of the deck, he sat and smoked. "This smoking no longer soothes. What business have I with this pipe? This thing is meant for quietness. I'll smoke no more—," he muttered.

He tossed the still lighted pipe into the sea. The fire hissed in the waves. The same instant the ship shot by the bubble the sinking pipe made. With slouched hat, Ahab paced the planks.

Next morning Stubb said to Flask, "Such a queer dream I never had. You know the old man's ivory leg; well, I dreamed he kicked me with it; and when I kicked back, upon my soul, my little man, I kicked my right leg right off! Ahab seemed a pyramid, and I, like a blazing fool, kept kicking at it. But now comes the greatest joke of the dream, Flask. While I was battering away at the pyramid, an old man takes me by the shoulders and turns me around.

" 'Halloa,' says I, 'what's the matter?'

" 'Look ye here,' says he; 'let's argue the insult. Captain Ahab kicked ye, didn't he?'

" 'Yes, he did,' says I.

" 'Well, then,' says he, 'wise Stubb, what have you to complain of? Didn't he kick with right good will? You were kicked by a great man, and with a beautiful ivory leg, Stubb. It's an honor. I consider it an honor. Listen, wise Stubb, ye were kicked by old Ahab, and made a wise man of. Account his kicks honors and on no account kick back, for you can't help yourself, wise Stubb. Don't you see that pyramid?' With that, he all of a sudden seemed somehow, in some fashion, to swim off into the air. I snored, rolled over, and there I was in my hammock! Now what do you think of that dream, Flask?"

"I don't know. It seems sort of foolish to me, though."

"Maybe, maybe. But it's made a wise man of me, Flask. D'ye see Ahab standing there sideways, looking over the stern? Well, the best thing you can do, Flask, is to let that old man alone. Never speak to him, whatever he says. Halloa! What's that he shouts? Hark!"

"Masthead, there! Look sharp, all of ye! There are whales hereabouts! If ye see a white one, split your lungs for him!"

"What d'ye think of that now, Flask? Ain't there a small drop of something queer about that, eh? A white whale, did ye mark that, man? Look ye—there's something special in the wind. Stand by for it, Flask. Ahab has that that's bloody on his mind. But, be quiet; he comes this way."

13 *The Cabin Table*

It is noon, and Dough-Boy, the steward, announces dinner to his lord and master, who was taking an observation of the sun. Then Ahab, for a moment seeming not to hear Dough-Boy, swings himself up to the deck, and says, "Dinner, Mr. Starbuck." Then Ahab disappears into the cabin. Then when Starbuck has every reason to suppose that Ahab is seated, Starbuck rouses, takes a few turns along the planks, and with some touch of pleasantness, says, "Dinner, Mr. Stubb," and goes down the scuttle. Stubb lounges about the rigging awhile, and then slightly shaking the main brace to see whether it be all right with that important rope, he likewise says, "Dinner, Mr. Flask," and follows after the others. Then a little while later, Flask enters King Ahab's presence.

Over his ivory-inlaid table Ahab presided like a mute, maned sea lion, surrounded by his warlike but still courteous cubs. In his proper turn, each officer waited to be served. They were as little children before Ahab, and these cabin meals were eaten in awful silence. Ahab did not forbid conversation; only he himself was dumb. What a relief it was to choking Stubb when a rat made a sudden racket in the hold below. And poor little Flask, he was the youngest son and little boy of this weary family party.

Peace and satisfaction, thought Flask, have forever

departed from my stomach. I am an officer, but how I wish I could fish a bit of old-fashioned beef in the forecastle as I used to when I was before the mast. Besides, if it were so that any mere sailor of the *Pequod* had a grudge against Flask, all that sailor had to do, in order to obtain ample vengeance, was to go aft at dinner time and get a peep at Flask through the cabin skylight, sitting silly and dumbfounded before awful Ahab.

Now Ahab and his three mates formed what may be called the first table in the *Pequod*'s cabin. After their departure, the canvas cloth was cleared, or rather restored to some hurried order by the steward. And then the three harpooneers were bidden to the feast. While their masters, the mates, seemed afraid of the sound of the hinges of their own jaws, the harpooneers chewed their food with such a relish that there was a report to it. They dined like lords; they filled their bellies all day like ships loading with spices. Such appetites had Queequeg and Tashtego, that to satisfy them Dough-Boy would bring out a great hunk of solid ox. And if he were not lively about it, if he did not go with a nimble hop-skip-and-jump, then Tashtego had an ungentlemanly way of hurrying him by darting a fork at his back, like a harpoon. And once Daggoo, to have fun with Dough-Boy, snatched him up bodily and thrust his head into a great empty wooden cuttingboard, while Tashtego, knife in hand, began pretending he was going to scalp him. After seeing the harpooneers furnished with all things they demanded, he would escape from them into his little pantry nearby, and fearfully peep out at them through the blinds of its doors until the meal was over.

When Dough-Boy would hear Tashtego singing out for him to produce himself in order that his bones might be picked, the steward all but shattered the crockery hanging around him in the pantry by his sudden fits of shaking. Nor did the whetstone which the harpooneers carried in their pockets for their lances and other weapons, with which whetstones at dinner they would sharpen their knives, at all help to calm poor Dough-Boy. In good time, though, to his great delight, the three salt-sea warriors would rise and depart.

But though these barbarians dined in the cabin and were supposed to live there, they were scarcely ever in it except at meal times and just before sleeping time, when they passed through it on the way to their own quarters.

In this one matter Ahab seemed like most American whale captains, who, as a set, have the opinion that by rights the ship's cabin belong to them, and that it is by courtesy that anyone else is, at any time, permitted there. So that, in real truth, the mates and harpooneers of the *Pequod* might more properly be said to have lived out of the cabin than in it. Nor did they lose much, for Ahab was a companion to no one. He lived in a world all his own.

14 *I Stand the Masthead*

It was during the more pleasant weather that my first turn at the masthead [1] came around. In most American vessels the mastheads are manned as soon as the vessel leaves port, even though she may have fifteen thousand miles and more to sail before reaching her hunting grounds. And if, after a three, four or five years' voyage she is drawing near home with anything empty in her, then her mastheads are kept manned to the last. There is always a chance of capturing one more whale.

The three masts are kept manned. from sunrise to sunset, the seamen taking their regular turns, and relieving each other every two hours. In the warm weather of the tropics it is exceedingly pleasant or even delightful to some men. There you stand a hundred feet above the silent decks, striding along the deep as if the masts were gigantic stilts. And beneath you and between your legs swim the hugest monsters of the sea. For the most part in this whaling life you hear no news, read no newspapers, hear of no afflictions, and are never troubled with the thought of what you shall have for dinner. All of your meals for three years and more are stored away, and your bill of fare is always the same.

In one of those southern whalemen, on a long three

---

[1] A lookout high above the top deck of the ship.

or four years voyage, as often happens, the sum of the various hours you spend at the masthead would amount to several entire months. Here, tossed about by the sea, the beginner feels about as cozy as he would standing on a bull's horns. I used to talk with Queequeg or anyone else off duty when I spent the long hours on the watch. Frankly, I admit that I was not a very good guard. I did not well observe all the whale ship's standing orders, "Keep your weather eye open, and sing out every time."

"Why, thou monkey," said a harpooneer to a lad like myself, "we're now hard upon three years and thou hast not raised a whale yet. Whales are as scarce as hen's teeth whenever thou are up there."

It was not a great while after the affair of the pipe, that one morning, shortly after breakfast, Ahab, as was his custom, came upon the deck. There most sea captains usually walk at that hour, as country gentlemen, after the same meal, take a few turns in the garden. Soon his steady, ivory stride was heard as he paced his old rounds upon planks so familiar to his tread that they were dented all over, like stones, with that peculiar mark of his walk. If you had gazed, too, upon that ribbed and dented brow, there also you would have seen still stranger footprints, the footprints of his one unsleeping, ever-pacing thought.

But on this occasion, those dents looked deeper, even as his nervous step that morning left a deeper mark. And so full of thought was Ahab that at every turn he made, you could almost see that thought turn in him as he turned, and pace in him as he paced.

It drew near the close of day. Suddenly he came to a halt, and inserting his bone leg into the auger hole there, and with one hand holding, he ordered Starbuck to send everybody to the upper deck.

"Sir!" said the mate, astonished at an order seldom or never given on shipboard except in some extraordinary case.

"Send everybody up," repeated Ahab. "Mastheads, there! Come down!"

When the ship's entire company was assembled, Ahab, looking like a storm coming up, darted his eyes among the crew. With bent head, he continued to pace. But the pacing did not last long. Stopping, he cried, "What do ye do when ye see a whale, men?"

"Sing out for him!" said a number of voices.

"Good!" said Ahab. "And what do ye do next, men?"

"Lower away, and after him!"

More and more strangely and fiercely glad and approving grew the face of the old man at every shout. The sailors gazed at each other as if wondering how it was that they had become so excited at Ahab's simple questions.

But they were all eagerness again as Ahab, now turning in his pivot-hole, spoke to them.

"All ye mastheaders have before now heard me give orders about a white whale. Look ye! D'ye see this Spanish ounce of gold?" He held up a broad bright coin to the sun. "It's a sixteen-dollar piece, men. D'ye see it? Mr. Starbuck, hand me yon hammer."

While the mate was getting the hammer, Ahab, without speaking, was slowly rubbing the gold piece against the skirts of his jacket, and lowly humming to himself.

Receiving the hammer from Starbuck, Ahab advanced toward the mainmast with the hammer uplifted in one hand, showing the gold with the other, and with a high raised voice said, "Whosoever of ye finds me a white-headed whale with a wrinkled brow and a crooked jaw; whosoever of ye finds me that white-headed whale, with three holes in him; look ye, whosoever of ye raises me that same white whale, he shall have this gold ounce, my boys!"

"Huzza! Huzza!" cried the seamen, as they watched Ahab nail the gold to the mast.

"It's a white whale, I say," resumed Ahab, as he threw down the hammer. "A white whale. Skin your eyes for him, men. Look sharp for white water. If ye see but a bubble, sing out."

All this while, Tashtego, Daggoo, and Queequeg had looked on with even more interest and surprise than the rest, and at the mention of the wrinkled brow and the crooked jaw, they acted as if they knew something about the white whale that Ahab had mentioned.

"Captain Ahab," said Tashtego, "that white whale must be the same that some call Moby Dick."

"Moby Dick?" shouted Ahab. "Do ye know the white whale then, Tash?"

"Does he fan-tail a little curious, sir, before he goes down?" asked Tashtego.

"And has he a curious spout, too," said Daggoo, "and mighty quick, Captain Ahab?"

"And he have one, two, tree—oh! good many iron in him hide, too, Captain," cried Queequeg, "all twisketee—." Queequeg was hunting for a word and screwing his hand round and round as though uncorking a bottle.

"Corkscrew!" cried Ahab. "Aye, Queequeg, the harpoons lie all twisted in him. Aye, Daggoo, his spout is a big one, like a whole shock of wheat, and white as a pile of our Nantucket wool after the great annual sheepshearing. Aye, Tashtego, he fan-tails like a split sail in a storm. Death and devils, men, it is Moby Dick ye have seen—Moby Dick—Moby Dick!"

"Captain Ahab," said Starbuck, who with Stubb and

Flask had been watching Ahab with increasing surprise. "Captain Ahab, I have heard of Moby Dick, but it was not Moby Dick who took off thy leg, was it?"

"Aye, Starbuck, aye, it was Moby Dick that took off my leg. Moby Dick brought me to this dead stump I stand on now. Aye, aye, it was the terrible white whale that made me crippled for ever and a day!" Then tossing both arms, he shouted out: "Aye, aye, and I'll chase him around Good Hope and the Horn and around Norway before I give him up. And this is what we have shipped for, men—to chase that white whale on both sides of land and over all sides of earth until he spouts black blood and dies! What say ye, men, will ye follow me now? I think ye do look brave."

"Aye, aye!" shouted the harpooneers and seamen, running closer to the excited old man. "A sharp eye for the white whale; a sharp eye for Moby Dick!"

"God bless ye," he seemed to half sob and half shout. "God bless ye, men. Steward, go draw rum, enough for everybody. But why so sad, Mr. Starbuck, do you not wish to chase the white whale? Do you not wish to seek Moby Dick?"

"I am game for his crooked jaw and for the jaws of Death, too, Captain Ahab, if it fairly comes in the way of the business we follow; but I came here to hunt whales, not help you get revenge. How many barrels of oil will Moby Dick yield even if we kill him, Captain Ahab? It would not fetch ye much in our Nantucket market!"

"Ahab smites his chest," whispered Stubb. "What's that for?"

"Revenge on a dumb brute!" cried Starbuck. "That is madness. To be angry with a dumb thing does not seem right, Captain Ahab."

"How can a prisoner reach outside except by thrusting through the wall?" shouted Ahab. "To me the

white whale is that wall. The crew, man, the crew! Are they not one and all with Ahab in this matter of the whale? You can not stand up against the whole crew, Starbuck."

"God keep me!—keep us all!" said Starbuck slowly.

"The drinks, the drinks!" cried Ahab. Receiving the cup, and then turning to the harpooneers, he ordered them to produce their weapons. Then ranging them before him, with their harpoons in their hands, while his three mates stood at his side with their lances, the rest of the ship's company forming a circle around the group, he stood for a minute watching every man of his crew. But those wild eyes met his as the bloodshot eyes of the prairie wolves meet the eyes of their leader before he rushes on at their head on the trail of the bison, only to fall into the hidden trap of the Indian.

"Drink and pass!" he cried, handing the heavy cup to the nearest seaman. "The crew alone now drink. Around with it, around! Well done; almost drained. Steward, refill. Watch now, my men. Ye harpooneers, stand there with your irons. Ye stout seamen, ring me in so that I may show you something my fishermen fathers did before me.

"Advance, ye mates! Cross your lances full before me. Drink, ye harpooneers! Drink and swear, ye men that man the whaleboats—Death to Moby Dick! God hunt us all if we do not hunt Moby Dick to his death!"

The long cups were lifted, and the sailors drank amid cries against Moby Dick, the White Whale. Starbuck became pale, turned and shivered at the thought of hunting Moby Dick and all the dangers that might arise from such a hunt. Once more, drinks were given to the crew before they scattered. Ahab then retired within his cabin.

15   *We Hear More of Moby Dick*

I, Ishmael, was one of the crew. My shouts had gone up with the rest, and I had agreed with them about killing Moby Dick. The stronger I shouted the more did I hammer and clinch my oath because of the dread in my soul. A wild feeling was in me, and Ahab's fight with Moby Dick seemed mine. With greedy ears I learned the history of that murderous monster against whom I and all the others had taken our oaths to kill.

For some time past, though at certain times only, the white whale, alone, had swum in seas most often visited by the sperm whale fishermen. But not all of them knew there was such a whale. Only a few of them had seen him, and the number who had actually and knowingly given battle to him was small indeed. For, owing to the large number of whale ships and the disorderly way in which they were sprinkled over all the seas, news of any kind seldom passed from ship to ship. Several vessels did battle a sperm whale of large size on several occasions, and I say that the whale in question must have been none other than Moby Dick.

Then there were those who, hearing of the white whale, by chance caught sight of him, and in the beginning every one of them had boldly tried to capture him. But so many accidents, some of which had caused death, had happened in the fights with Moby Dick, that a great many whalemen became afraid to seek him.

Wild rumors, too, made Moby Dick more terrible than he really was, for such is the case of rumors on the sea even more than on the land.

However, there were some who even in the face of these things were ready to give chase to Moby Dick, and a still greater number would not flee from a fight with him. In the minds of some seamen there was the belief that Moby Dick was everywhere and that he had actually been fought in two places at the same time.

The hidden ways of the sperm whale beneath the surface remain secret, and some have said that once underneath the water, the whale travels with vast swiftness.

It is a thing well known to both American and English whale ships that some whales have been captured far north in the Pacific, in whose bodies have been found the barbs of harpoons placed there in the Greenland seas. Nor is it to be denied that in some of these instances it has been said that the length of time between the two fights could not have been more than a few days.

Since the white whale had escaped alive so many times, many seamen thought that he not only was everywhere but that he could not be killed, since, though groves of spears had been planted in his flanks, he would still swim away unharmed.

It was not so much his size that made him look different from other sperm whales, but he had a peculiar snow-white wrinkled forehead and a high white hump. These were his prominent features, the things by which he was known at a long distance even in the unlimited seas. The rest of his body was so streaked, spotted, and marbled with the same white color that he was called the white whale, a name that was especially fitting for him when he was seen gliding at high noon through a dark blue sea.

When swimming before his hunters, Moby Dick had several times been known to turn around suddenly and, bearing down upon them, either stave their boats to splinters or drive them back in fear to their ship. Already several men had been killed while hunting the great whale, although not much was said about it on shore since such things were common in whale fishery.

In Captain Ahab's fight with Moby Dick, there were three boats crushed, and oars and men were whirling in the water. Ahab, seizing the lifeline-knife from his broken boat, dashed at the whale, blindly seeking with a six-inch blade to kill the monster. And then it was that suddenly sweeping his sickle-shaped lower jaw beneath him, Moby Dick had ripped away Ahab's leg as a mower cuts a blade of grass in the field. Is there any wonder then, ever since that fight in which Ahab almost lost his life, that he desired to kill the whale?

After he had lost his leg, Ahab was forced to turn homeward, and for long days and weeks he lay in terrible pain. At times during the long voyage he was raving mad. And though without a leg, he had so much strength in his chest that his mates were forced to tie him fast in his hammock. Thus tied, he swung to the mad rockings of the gales. When the warmer oceans were reached, Ahab improved and he came forth from his dark den into the blessed light and air. When he bore that firm face, however pale, and issued his calm orders once again, his mates thanked God that his madness was now gone. But it was not gone, and Ahab, in his mind, raved on. Human madness is sometimes like a cat. When you think it is gone, it may reappear again. But so well did Ahab keep to himself his desire to kill the white whale that when he stepped ashore at last, no Nantucketer noticed there was any difference in him except his ivory leg.

So it is now clear to me that Ahab, with his mad desire to destroy the white whale, had purposely sailed upon the present voyage with the sole purpose of hunting the white whale. Had any of his friends half dreamed of what he was going to do, they would not have permitted him to take the *Pequod* on such a voyage. They were sending the ship out to make money from whale oil, but he was out to kill the white whale.

Here, then, was this gray-headed old man, at the head of a crew, too, seeking a whale around the world. At times Ahab's hate seemed almost the crew's, and the white whale was as much their foe as his. But I could see nothing in Moby Dick but the deadliest danger.

A short time after Ahab had nailed the gold to the mast, some of the members of the crew heard strange noises from the lower decks. "Hist! Did you hear that noise, Cabaco?" The speaker was Archy, who was one of the seamen on watch. There was a fair moonlight, and the seamen were standing in a line passing buckets to fill the scuttle butt.[1] Standing for the most part on Ahab's quarter-deck, they were careful not to speak or rustle their feet. From hand to hand, the buckets went in deepest silence, broken only by the occasional flap of a sail, and the steady hum of the unceasingly advancing keel.

It was in the midst of this quietness that Archy had whispered the above words to Cabaco. "Take the

---

[1] A butt is a large barrel, and a scuttle is a small opening in a ship's deck.

bucket, will ye, Archy? What noise d'ye mean?" said Cabaco.

"There it is again. Don't you hear it? A cough—it sounded like a cough."

"Cough be damned! Pass along that return bucket."

"There again—there it is! It sounds like two or three sleepers turning over, now!"

"It's the three soaked biscuits ye eat for supper turning over inside of ye—nothing else. Look to the bucket!"

"Say what ye will, shipmate, but I've sharp ears. Grin away. We'll see what turns up. Hark ye, Cabaco, there is somebody down in the after hold that has not been seen on deck, and I am pretty sure old Ahab knows something about it, too. I heard Stubb tell Flask on one morning watch that there was something of that sort in the wind."

Had you followed Captain Ahab down into his cabin after the storm that took place after he had pledged his crew to follow Moby Dick, you would have seen him go to a locker and bring out a large wrinkled roll of yellowish sea charts and spread them on his screwed-down table. Then seating himself before the table he studied the various lines and shadings which there met his eye, and with slow but steady pencil, he traced routes over the spaces. At times he would refer to piles of logbooks, in which were set down the seasons and places in which on former voyages of other ships sperm whales had been captured or seen.

While he was doing this, the heavy pewter lamp hanging in chains over his head continually rocked with the motion of the ship and threw shifting gleams and shadows of lines upon his wrinkled brow. It almost seemed that while he himself was marking out lines

and courses on the wrinkled charts, some invisible pencil also was tracing lines and courses upon the deeply
marked chart of his forehead.

But it was not only this night that, alone in his
cabin, Ahab went over his charts. Almost every night
they were brought out, and almost every night some
pencil marks were erased and others were made. For with
the charts of all oceans before him, Ahab tried to make
Moby Dick's destruction more certain.

Now, to anyone not fully acquainted with the habits
of whales, it might seem like a hopeless task to find one

whale in the watery wastes. But not so did it seem to Ahab, who knew the sets of all tides and currents, and was able to know just where the sperm whale fed. He also knew the best seasons for hunting him.

When making a passage from one feeding ground to another, the sperm whales mostly swim in veins: courses which they follow exactly. The vein is generally some few miles in width, but is never too wide not to be seen from the ship's masthead. Thus at particular seasons, within that breadth and along that path, the traveling whales may be looked for with great confidence. Ahab, then, could go from feeding ground to feeding ground; and even in traveling from one to the other, there was always a chance of meeting Moby Dick.

Though sperm whales, which travel in groups, have their regular seasons for particular grounds, yet in general you can not be certain that the herds that were in such and such a place this year will be there next season. However, there are records to prove that they have, in some cases, returned.

So it is with aged sperm whales, which travel alone. Moby Dick had in a former year been seen, for example, in the Indian Ocean or in Volcano Bay on the Japanese coast. Yet one could not be certain that were the *Pequod* to visit either of these spots the following season that Moby Dick would be found there. So too, it was with some other feeding grounds, where he had at times been seen. But all these seemed to be only stopping places, not his regular home. For several years Moby Dick had been seen in one certain spot, and it was there, too, that most of the deadly fights had taken place, and it was there that Ahab had lost his leg.

Now the *Pequod* had sailed from Nantucket at the very time that Moby Dick had often been in his usual spot, and there was no way possible for the ship to reach these waters in time. Therefore, it would be necessary to wait for the next season. Yet, the time of the *Pequod*'s sailing probably had been correctly chosen by Ahab. There were 365 days, a whole year, before he could really expect the whale, but he would spend his time hunting in waters where there was still some chance that Moby Dick might be found.

Even in the boundless ocean, Moby Dick, with his snow-white hump, could easily be recognized when found. "And have I not traced the route of the whale?" Ahab would say to himself after looking over his charts until long after midnight. Here his mad mind would run on in a breathless race, and in the open air of the deck he would seek to recover his strength. Often Ahab had dreams of chasing the white whale, and sometimes, uttering a wild cry, he would burst from his stateroom as though escaping from a bed on fire.

To say something more about the habits of whales and of Ahab's chance of finding Moby Dick, I might explain that I have personally known three instances where a whale, after receiving a harpoon, has escaped only to be caught later by the same hand. In one of these cases, more than three years had gone by before the whale was harpooned the second time. During that time, the whale must have been on his travels, and had been around the world three times. But this man and this whale came together again, and the one killed the other. I say I, myself, have known three instances like this. That is, in two of them I saw the whales struck, and, upon the second attack, saw the two irons taken from the dead fish. In the three-year instance, it so happened that I was in the boat both times, and the last time I recognized a huge mole under the whale's eye, one which I had seen three years before. I say three years, but I am pretty sure it was more than that.

Though most men have some ideas of the dangers of whale fishing, they do not know how often deaths actually do occur. One reason, perhaps, is that not one in fifty of the deaths ever finds a public record at home. Do you suppose that that poor fellow there, who this moment perhaps was caught by the whale-line off New Guinea and was carried down to the bottom of the sea, will have his name in the newspaper you will read tomorrow at your breakfast? No, because the mails are very irregular between here and New Guinea. In fact, did you ever hear what might be called regular news direct or indirect from New Guinea? Yet I tell you that upon one particular voyage which I made to the Pacific, we met thirty different ships, every one of which had had a death by a whale, some of them more than one, and three that each lost a boat's crew. Then be careful with your lamps and candles! Every gallon you burn has at least one drop of man's blood spilled for it.

The sperm whale is in some cases so powerful that he has been known to destroy and sink a large ship. In the year 1820, in the ship *Essex*, Captain Pollard of Nantucket was cruising in the Pacific Ocean. One day she saw spouts, lowered her boats, and gave chase to a large number of sperm whales. Before long, after several of the whales had been wounded, a very large whale, escaping the boats, suddenly bore directly down upon the ship. Dashing his forehead against her hull, he so stove her in, that in less than ten minutes she settled down and fell over. Not a surviving plank of her has been seen since. After the severest exposure, part of the crew reached the land in their boats.

Being returned home at last, Captain Pollard once more sailed for the Pacific in command of another ship, but the gods shipwrecked him again upon unknown rocks and breakers. For the second time his ship was lost, and he has never gone to sea again. And this day Captain Pollard is a resident of Nantucket.

I will now refer you to a story told by a Captain Langsdorff, who in his seventeenth chapter says: "By the thirteenth of May our ship was ready to sail, and the next day we were out in the open sea. The weather was very clear and fine, but it was so cold that we had to keep on our fur clothing. For some days we had very little wind, and it was not until the nineteenth that a brisk gale from the northwest sprang up. An uncommon large whale, the body of which was larger than the ship itself, lay almost on the surface of the water, but was not seen by anyone on board until the moment when the ship, which was in full sail, was almost upon him, and it was impossible to keep from striking the monster. We were thus placed in great danger, as this huge creature, pushing up its back, raised the ship three feet, at least, out of the water. The masts reeled and the sails fell, while we who were below all sprang instantly upon the deck, believing we had struck a rock. Instead of this we saw the monster swimming silently away. The captain started the pumps immediately to see whether the vessel had received any damage from the shock, but we found that very happily it had escaped undamaged."

In a book of old-fashioned adventure, Lionel Wafer tells another story that I must pass along: "About four o'clock in the morning, when we were about one hundred fifty leagues from the mainland of America, our ship felt a terrible shock, which so frightened our men that every one of them began to prepare for death. And, indeed, the shock was so sudden and violent that we took it for granted the ship had struck a rock; but when we examined the water, we found no ground underneath the ship. The suddenness of the shock made the guns leap in their carriages, and several of the men were shaken out of their hammocks. Captain Davis, who lay with his head on a gun, was thrown out of his cabin. Lionel says the shock was probably due to an earthquake, but I should not much wonder that in the darkness of that early hour of the morning the shock was after all caused by an unseen whale bumping the ship from underneath."

I might give several more examples, one way or another known to me, of the great power and fighting strength of the sperm whale. In more than one instance, he has been known not only to chase the boats back to their ships but also to pursue the ship itself and to withstand all the lances hurled at him from its decks. The English ship *Pusie Hall* can tell a story on that. And as for the strength of the sperm whale, let me say that there have been examples where the lines attached to a running sperm whale have, in a calm, been tied to the ship, and the whale has towed the ship through the water as a horse walks off with a cart. Again it is very often seen that if a sperm whale once struck is allowed to fight back, he then often tries to destroy the men in the boats. Upon being attacked, he will often open his mouth and keep it open for many minutes.

In the sixth century, according to an old account, there was captured near Constantinople a great sea monster which had destroyed vessels in those waters for a period of more than fifty years. What kind of monster he was is not explained, but he must have been a whale, and I think he must have been a sperm whale.

16 *We Lower*[1] *for Whales*

To Captain Ahab the voyage of the *Pequod* had only one purpose—to capture Moby Dick—and he would sacrifice everything, including his crew, if necessary, for that one purpose. To do this, Ahab must use tools, and of all tools used, men are most likely to get out of order. He knew that for the moment Starbuck was in his power, but he knew that Starbuck might lead the crew against him. Ahab knew, too, that sailors are sometimes unreliable. Thus Ahab pretended that the voyage was not different from other Nantucket whaling voyages, and told his men always to keep a sharp lookout for all whales.

It was a cloudy, sultry afternoon. The seamen were lazily lounging about the decks or vacantly gazing over into the lead-colored waters. Queequeg and I were weaving a sword mat, to be used in our boat, as dreaminess reigned over all the ship and all over the sea. Thus we were weaving and weaving away when I started at a sound so strange, long-drawn, and musically wild and unearthly that my weaving fell from my hand, and I stood gazing up at the clouds from where I heard a voice.

High aloft in the cross-trees was Tashtego. His body was reaching eagerly forward, his hand stretched

---

[1] Let down boats.

out like a wand, and at brief intervals he continued his cries.

"There she blows! there! there! she blows! she blows!"

"Where-away?"

"About two miles off, a school of them!"

Instantly there was action everywhere.

The sperm whale blows as a clock ticks, and it is by this regular blowing that whalemen can distinguish the whale from other fish.

"Quick, steward!" cried Ahab. "Time! Time!" Dough-Boy hurried below, glanced at the watch, and reported the exact minute to Ahab.

The ship was now kept away from the wind, and she went gently rolling before it. Tashtego reported that the whales had gone down, and we expected to see them again directly in front of the ship.

But at this critical moment there was a sudden cry that took every eye. With a start all glared at dark Ahab, who was surrounded by five sailors that the crew had not seen before. These five had caused some of the noises that the men had heard and could not account for. These were the men that had been seen slyly going aboard just before Queequeg and I had left on the voyage at Nantucket.

The five, who seemed like ghosts, were flitting on the other side of the deck and were casting loose the tackles and bands of the boat that swung there. The boat had always been called a spare boat, though it was called the captain's because it was so near his quarters. While yet the wondering ship's company were gazing upon these strangers, Ahab cried out to the old man at their head, "All ready there, Fedallah?"

"Ready," was his answer.

"Lower away then. D'ye hear?" he shouted across the deck. "Lower away there, I say."

Such was the thunder of his voice that the men sprang over the rail, the three boats dropped into the sea, and the sailors, goat-like, leaped down the rolling ship's side into the tossed boats below.

Hardly had they pulled out from beside the ship when a fourth boat, with the five strangers rowing Ahab, showed itself. Ahab, standing erect, loudly ordered Starbuck, Stubb, and Flask to spread themselves widely, so as to cover a large expanse of water. But with all their eyes again riveted upon Fedallah and his crew, the men on the other boats did not obey the command.

"Captain Ahab—?" said Starbuck.

"Spread yourselves," cried Ahab. "Give way, all four boats. Thou, Flask, pull out more with the wind."

Yes, yes, sir," answered Flask. "There she blows right ahead, boys. Lay back! Never mind the strangers, Archy."

"Oh, I don't mind 'em, sir," said Archy. "I knew it all before now. Didn't I hear 'em? And didn't I tell Cabaco here of it? What say ye, Cabaco? They are stowaways, Mr. Flask."

"Pull, pull, my children. Pull, my little ones," said Stubb to his crew, some of whom showed signs of uneasiness. "Why don't you break your backbones, my boys? What is it you stare at? Those chaps in yonder boat? They are only five more hands come to help us. Never mind from where—the more the merrier. Why don't you snap your oars, you rascals? Bite something, you dogs! That's it; that's it! Long and strong. Stop snoring, ye sleepers, and pull." Stubb, although he urged with strong words his men to pull, never became angry. And good leader that he was, his men had much respect for him and obeyed.

Starbuck's and Stubb's boats came close together, and Stubb said, "Mr. Starbuck, a word with ye, sir, if ye please!"

"Holloa!" returned Starbuck.

"What think ye of those strangers, sir?" said Stubb.

"Smuggled on board, somehow, before the ship sailed. A sad business, Mr. Stubb, but never mind. Perhaps it's all for the best. Let your crew pull strong, come what will. There are barrels of sperm oil ahead, Mr. Stubb, and that's what ye came for. Sperm, sperm's the play! That at least is duty, duty and profit, hand in hand!"

"Aye, I thought as much," said Stubb. "As soon as I saw them, I thought so. Aye, and that's what he went into the after hold for so often, as Dough-Boy long suspected. They were hidden down there. The white whale is at the bottom of it. Well, well, so be it! Can't be helped! All right! Give way, men! It ain't the white whale today! Give way!"

Now the appearance of the five strangers at the lowering of the boat from the deck had made the crew a bit superstitious. However, they were not so afraid as might have been expected in such a situation, because Archy, although not believed by all, had told of hearing the strange noises. For me, I silently recalled the mysterious shadows I had seen creeping on board the *Pequod* during the dim Nantucket dawn. I also thought about Elijah.

"Every man look out along his oars!" cried Starbuck. "Thou, Queequeg, stand up!" Nimbly springing up on the triangular raised box in the bow, the savage stood erect there, and with intensely eager eyes gazed off toward the spot where the whales had been last seen.

Stubb, as was his custom, drew his pipe from his hatband. He loaded it and rammed home the loading with his thumb-end, but hardly had he struck the match across the rough sandpaper of his hand when Tashtego, his harpooneer, suddenly dropped like light to his seat, crying out in a quick frenzy of hurry, "Down, down all, and give way! There they are!"

Beneath a thin layer of water the whales were swimming. All four boats were now in keen pursuit of that one spot of troubled water and air. "Pull, pull, my good boys," said Starbuck in the lowest possible whisper to his men.

How different was the loud Flask: "Sing out and say something, my hearties. Roar and pull, my thunderbolts!" And so shouting, he pulled his hat from his head, stamped up and down on it, picked it up, and then whirled it far out upon the sea. Finally, he fell to rearing and plunging in the boat's stern like a crazed colt from the prairie.

"Look at that chap, now," said Stubb, who, with his unlighted short pipe, followed after. "He's got fits, that Flask has. Pull, babes, pull, all. But what the devil are you hurrying about? Softly, softly, and steadily, my men. Only pull and keep pulling, nothing more. Crack all your backbones and bite your knives in two—that's all. Take it easy—why don't ye take it easy, I say?"

Meanwhile, all the boats tore on. It was a sight full of quick wonder! There was the vast swell of the powerful sea as well as the sight of the ivory *Pequod* bearing down upon her boats with outstretched sails like a hen running after her chickens. All this was thrilling. The young soldier, marching into his first battle, can have no stranger or stronger feelings than does the man who for the first time finds himself pulled into the charmed, churned circle of the hunted sperm whale.

The dancing white water made by the chase could be seen more and more easily because of cloud shadows on the sea. The jets of vapor showed to both right and left, and the whales seemed to be separating. The boats pulled more apart, Starbuck giving chase to three whales.

"Give way, men," whispered Starbuck. "There is still time to kill fish yet before yonder storm comes. There's white water again! Close to! Spring!"

Soon after, two cries, one after the other, on each side of us told us that the other two boats had thrown harpoons into whales. But hardly were they overheard when, with a lightning-like whisper, Starbuck said, "Stand up!" and Queequeg, harpoon in hand, sprang to his feet.

Although not one of the oarsmen was then facing the danger that lay so close to them ahead, they knew that the time of peril was close at hand. They heard, too, a sound as of fifty elephants. Meanwhile, the boat was still booming through the mist, the waves curling and hissing around us like the erected crests of enraged serpents.

"That's his hump. There, there, give it to him!" whispered Starbuck. A short rushing sound leaped out of the boat; it was the darted iron of Queequeg. Then came a pull which shot the boat forward. The whole crew were half without breath as they were tossed helter-skelter into the white curdling cream of the storm. Storm, whale, and harpoon were all mixed together, and the whale, who had not been hit well by the iron, escaped.

Though completely swamped, the boat was nearly unharmed. Swimming around it, we picked up the floating oars and finally tumbled back into our places. There we sat up to our knees in the sea, the water covering every rib and plank.

The wind increased to a howl, the waves dashed together, the whole storm roared, forked, and crackled around us like a white fire upon the prairie. We tried to call the other boats, but we could not make them hear. Meanwhile, the mist grew darker with the coming of night, and no sign of the ship could be seen. The rising sea stopped all attempts to get the water from the boat, and the oars were useless except for life preservers. However, after many failures, Starbuck managed to light the lamp in the lantern, and, tying it on a pole, handed it to Queequeg.

Wet, drenched through, shivering cold, and thinking we had lost the *Pequod* forever, we lifted up our eyes as the dawn came on. The mist still spread over the sea, and the empty lantern lay crushed in the bottom of the boat. Suddenly Queequeg started to his feet, putting his hand behind his ear. We all heard a faint creaking, sounding something like ropes. The sound came nearer and nearer, and finally the thick mists were dimly parted by a huge vague form. Frightened, we all sprang into the sea as the ship at last loomed into view.

We saw the abandoned boat tossed upon the waves, and then it was rolled over by the large hull of the ship. Then the boat was seen no more until it came up astern. Again we swam for it, were dashed against it by the seas, and were at last taken up and safely landed on board.

There we learned that before the storm had arrived, the other boats had cut loose from their whales and returned to the ship in good time. The ship had given us up, but was still searching, hoping to find an oar or a lance pole from our boat.

"Queequeg," said I when they had dragged me, the last man, to the deck, and I was still shaking myself in my jacket to fling off the water, "Queequeg, does this sort of thing often happen?" Without being very much surprised, though soaked just like me, he gave me to understand that such things did often happen.

"Mr. Stubb," said I, turning to that worthy, who, buttoned up in his oil jacket, was now calmly smoking his pipe in the rain, "Mr. Stubb, I think I have heard you say that of all the whalemen you ever met, our chief mate, Mr. Starbuck, is by far the most careful when going after whales. I suppose, then, that going after whales with a storm coming up is being careful?"

"Certain. I've lowered for whales from a leaking ship in a storm off Cape Horn."

Then considering what a devil's chase I was in on the voyage, one which concerned the white whale, I thought it was so dangerous that I might as well go below and make my will. "Queequeg," said I, "come along. You shall be my lawyer."

17 *A Spirit-Spout Lures Us*

"Who would have thought it, Flask!" cried Stubb. "If I had but one leg, you would not catch me in a boat, unless maybe to stop the plughole with my timber toe. Oh, he's a wonderful old man!"

"I don't think it so strange, after all, on that account," said Flask. "If his leg were off at the hip, now, it would be a different thing. That would disable him, but he has one knee and a good part of the other left, you know."

"I don't know that, my little man. I never yet saw him kneel."

Those persons who know a great deal about whaling often argue whether, considering the importance of the life of the captain to the voyage, it is right for him to risk himself in the active dangers of the chase. The pursuit of whales is always under great and extraordinary difficulties, and is it wise for any crippled man to enter a whaleboat in the hunt? The joint owners of the *Pequod* must have plainly thought not.

Ahab well knew that although his friends at home would think little of his entering a boat for the sake of being near the scene of action and giving his orders in person; yet for Captain Ahab to have a boat in the hunt and to be supplied with five extra men had never entered the heads of the owners of the *Pequod*. But Ahab had not asked for a boat's crew from the owners, and neither had he told them what he intended to do. He had hidden aboard, as was now clear to everybody, the five sailors who were to handle his own boat. Until Archy's discovery, no one had suspected such a thing, although Ahab's interest in one of the spare boats and his strengthening and equipping it, might have aroused curiosity.

But everybody thought these preparations by Ahab were made with Moby Dick in mind, for he had already said he intended to hunt that monster in person. But this did not cause anyone to suspect that there was another crew to be assigned to the spare boat. However, since sailors are used to unusual things, the excitement of Ahab's hidden crew soon died away. On a whaling boat the devil himself might climb up the side and step down into the cabin to chat with the captain, and it would not create any unusual excitement in the forecastle.

Days, weeks passed, and under easy sail, the ivory *Pequod* had slowly slipped across four cruising-grounds; that off the Azores; off the Cape de Verdes; off the mouth of the Rio de la Plata; and the Carrol Ground, an un-staked, watery locality southerly from St. Helena.

It was while gliding through these latter waters that one moonlight night, when all the waves rolled by like scrolls of silver, that a silvery jet was seen far in advance of the white bubbles at the bow. Fedallah first saw it, for on these moonlight nights it was his custom to mount the mainmast head and stand a lookout there, as if it had been day. And yet, though herds of whales were seen by night, not one whaleman in a hundred would go after them.

Walking the deck with quick, side-lunging strides, Ahab commanded that the best man in the ship take the helm. Then, with every masthead manned, the piled-up craft rolled down before the wind. And had you watched Ahab's face that night, you would have thought that in him two different things were warring. While his one live leg made lively echoes along the deck, every stroke of his dead limb sounded like a coffin tap. On life and death this old man walked. But though the ship so swiftly sped, and though every eye, like arrows, the eager glances shot, yet the silvery jet was seen no more that night. Every sailor swore he saw it once, but not a second time.

The midnight spout had almost grown a forgotten thing, when, some days after, at the same silent hour, it was again announced. But upon making sail to overtake it, the crew found it once more disappeared as if it had never been. And so it served us night after night until no one noticed it very much. It would mysteriously jet into the clear moonlight, or starlight, as the case might be, and then disappear again for one whole day, or two days or three. Some of the sailors swore that the jets were those of Moby Dick, who was leading the ship on in order that he might finally turn upon the *Pequod* and destroy it in the farthest and most savage seas.

At last, when the ship turned to the eastward, the Cape winds began howling around us, and we rose and fell upon the long, troubled seas that are there. Close to our bows, strange forms in the water darted hither and thither before us, while thick in our rear flew sea ravens. And every morning, perched on our stays, rows of these birds were seen. And in spite of our hootings, they would cling to the ropes as though they deemed our ship to be without a crew.

Cape of Good Hope, do they call ye? Soon we found ourselves in that angry sea. With his ivory leg

inserted into its hole, Ahab would for hours and hours stand gazing dead to windward, while occasional sleet or snow would all but freeze his eyelashes together. Meanwhile, the crew, driven from the forward part of the ship by the stormy seas that burstingly broke over its bows, stood in a line along the bulwarks in the waist.[1] And the better to guard against the leaping waves, each man had slipped himself into a sort of bowline secured to the rail, in which he swung as in a loosened belt. Few or no words were spoken, and the silent ship, as if manned by painted sailors in wax, day after day tore on through all the swift madness and gladness of the waves.

Even when he was tired from watching the storm, Ahab would not seek rest in his hammock. Never could Starbuck forget the look on the old man's face when one night he saw him, with closed eyes, sitting straight in his floor-screwed chair. On the table beside Ahab lay unrolled one of those charts of tides and currents which have previously been spoken of. His lantern swung from his tightly clenched hand. Though the body was erect, the head was thrown back so that the closed eyes were pointed toward the needle of the tell-tale[2] that swung from a beam in the ceiling.

"Terrible old man!" thought Starbuck. "Sleeping in this gale, but never departing from his purpose."

---

[1] The central part of the ship.
[2] The cabin compass is called the tell-tale, because without going to the compass at the helm, the Captain, while below, can inform himself of the course of the ship.

18 We Meet Other Whalers and Hear More of Moby Dick

Southeastward from the Cape, off the distant Crozetts, a good place for finding right whales, we came upon another ship, the *Goney* or *Albatross*. As she slowly drew near, from my lofty perch at the foremast head, I had a good view of that sight so remarkable to a beginner in the far ocean fisheries—a whaler at sea and long absent from home.

The ship was bleached white like the skeleton of a dead walrus. All down her sides were long channels of reddened rust, and all her spars and rigging were like the thick branches of trees covered with frost. Only her lower sails were set. A wild sight it was to see her long-bearded men watching from those three mastheads. They seemed clad in the skins of beasts, so torn and patched were the clothes that had survived nearly four years on the sea.

"Ship ahoy! Have ye seen the white whale?" Ahab shouted to the captain of the *Goney*.

But as the strange captain, leaning over the bulwarks, was in the act of putting the trumpet to his mouth, it somehow fell from his hand into the sea, and he could not make himself heard. Meanwhile his ship was still increasing the distance between us. Ahab paused for a moment—it almost seemed as though he would have lowered a boat to board the stranger had not the threatening wind stopped him. But he again

seized his trumpet, knowing that the strange vessel was a Nantucketer and shortly bound for home, and shouted, "Ahoy there! This is the *Pequod*, bound round the world! Tell them to address all future letters to the Pacific Ocean! And this time three years from now if I am not at home, tell them to address them to—."

Then turning to the steersman, who had cut down her speed, Ahab cried out in his old lion voice, "Up helm! Keep her going round the world!"

The seeming reason why Ahab did not go on board of the whaler was the high wind. But even had this not been the case, he would not after all, perhaps, have boarded her had they told him by shouting they had not seen the white whale. As it turned out, he cared not to spend five minutes with any stranger captain if he could not tell him something about Moby Dick.

How much more natural that under such circumstances these ships should come close and make sociable contact. For the long absent ship, the outward-bounder, perhaps, has letters on board. At any rate, she will be sure to let her have some papers of a date a year or two later than the last one on her blurred and thumb-worn files. And in return for the papers, the outward-bound ship would receive the latest whaling news from the places to which she is traveling. This meeting of ships holds true even of whaling vessels crossing each other's track, even though they are equally long absent from home. For one of them may have received a transfer of letters from a third ship, and some of those letters may be for the people of the ship she now meets.

Nor would the difference of country matter much so long as both parties speak one language, as is the case with Americans and English. So, then, we see that of all ships sailing the seas, the whalers have most reason to be sociable. And they are so. Merchant ships passing each other in the mid-Atlantic will often pass on without so much as a single word. As for men-of-war,[1] when they chance to meet at sea, they first go through such a string of silly bowings and scrapings that there does not seem to be much hearty goodwill and brotherly love about it at all. And slave ships meeting are in such a hurry they run away from each other as soon as possible. And as for pirates, when they chance to cross each other's crossbones, their first greeting is "How many skulls?"—the same way that whalers say, "How many barrels?"

But look at the godly, honest, sociable, free-and-easy whaler! What does the whaler do when she meets another whaler in any sort of decent weather? She has

---

[1] Men-of-war are fighting ships.

a gam with the other crew. But what is a gam? You might look in a dozen dictionaries and never find the word. However, this word has been in constant use among some fifteen thousand true born Yankees. A gam is a social meeting of two or more whale ships, which, after exchanging greetings, exchange visits by boat's crews. The two captains remain for a time on board of one ship and the two chief mates on the other.

The Cape of Good Hope, as well as all the watery region round about there, is much like some noted four corners of a great highway where you meet more travelers than in any other part. And it was not very long after meeting the *Goney* that another homeward-bound whaleman, the *Town-Ho*, was met. In the short gam that followed, she gave us strong news of Moby Dick.

"It was just between daybreak and sunrise," one of the *Town-Ho* crew told us, "when we were washing down the decks, when the watch shouted out, 'There she rolls! There she rolls!' What a whale! It was Moby Dick.

" 'The white whale! The white whale!' was the cry from the captain, mates, and harpooneers, who, unafraid, were eager to capture so famous and precious a fish. Four boats were lowered, and finally a harpoon was attached to the white whale. All of a sudden the boat from which the harpoon had been thrown struck something like a sunken ledge, and, turning over, spilled out the standing mate. That instant, as he fell on the whale's slippery back, the boat righted and was dashed aside by the swell. The mate, tossed over into the sea at the side of the whale, sought to remove himself from the eye of Moby Dick. But the whale seized the swimmer between his jaws; and rearing high up with him, plunged headlong into the seas again and went down."

19 *We Find the Great Live Squid*

Steering northeastward from the Crozetts, we fell in with vast meadows of brit, the small yellow substance upon which the right whale largely feeds. For miles and miles it was around us, and we seemed to be sailing through boundless fields of ripe and golden wheat.

On the second day numbers of right whales, with open jaws, were seen. As morning mowers, who side by side slowly and seethingly advance their scythes, these monsters swam, making a strange, grassy, cutting sound, and leaving behind them endless strips of blue upon the yellow sea.

Slowly wading through the meadows of brit, the *Pequod* still held on her way northeastward toward the island of Java. And still, at various times, in the silvery night, the lonely jet would be seen.

But one still morning a strange sight was seen by Daggoo from the mainmast head. In the distance a great white mass lazily rose. It glistened for a moment, and then sank. Then once more it arose and silently gleamed. It seemed not a whale; and yet, "Is this Moby Dick?" thought Daggoo. Again the thing went down, but on its reappearance once more, Daggoo yelled out, "There! there again! there she breaches![1] right ahead! The white whale, the white whale!"

[1] Breaks the waves.

Upon this shout, the seamen rushed to their posts, as in swarming time bees rush to a bough. Bareheaded in the hot sun, Ahab stood watching Daggoo, with one hand pushed far behind ready to give orders. And as soon as the white mass was seen again, Ahab gave orders for lowering. The four boats were soon on the water, Ahab's in advance, and all swiftly pulling toward their prey. Soon it went down, and while we were waiting for its reappearance, in the same spot where it sank, once more it slowly rose. Almost forgetting for the moment all thoughts of Moby Dick, we now gazed at the most wondrous animal which the secret seas have shown to man.

A vast pulpy mass, quite long and wide and cream-colored, lay floating on the water, with many long arms coming out from its center and curling and twisting like a nest of snakes. It had no face or front. With a slow sucking sound it slowly disappeared again, and Starbuck, still gazing at the waters where it had sunk, with a wild voice said, "Almost rather had I seen Moby Dick and fought him than to have seen thee, thou white ghost!"

"What was it, sir?" asked Flask.

"The great live squid, which, they say, few whale ships ever saw and returned to their ports to tell of it."

But Ahab said nothing, and turning his boat, he sailed back to the vessel, the rest silently following.

So seldom is the great live squid seen that sailors say it is the largest thing alive in the ocean, yet very few of them know its true nature and form, yet they believe it to furnish the sperm whale with his only food. For though other kinds of whales find their food above water, and may be seen by man in the act of feeding, the sperm whale obtains his food in unknown zones below the surface, and no one actually knows of what his food consists. At times, when closely pursued, he will vomit what are supposed to be the detached arms of the squid, some of them exceeding twenty and thirty feet in length. Seamen fancy that the monster to which these arms belonged ordinarily clings by them to the bed of the ocean, and that the sperm whale, unlike other kinds of whales, is supplied with teeth in order to attack and tear it.

20 Stubb Kills a Whale

Although to Starbuck the squid was something in the way of a bad warning, to Queequeg it was quite a different object. "When you see-e squid," said the savage, sharpening his harpoon in the bow of his boat, "then you quick see a sperm whale."

The next day was exceedingly still and sultry, and with nothing special to do, the *Pequod*'s crew could hardly resist going to sleep. For this part of the Indian Ocean through which we were then voyaging is not what whalemen call a lively ground. That is, it affords fewer glimpses of porpoises, dolphins, flying fish, and other kinds of fish than those off the Rio de la Plata or the inshore ground off Peru.

It was my turn to stand at the foremast head. And with my shoulders leaning against the sails, to and fro I idly swayed in what seemed an enchanted air. Before forgetfulness altogether came over me, I noticed that the other watchmen were also drowsy. At last all three of us lifelessly swung from the spars, and for every swing that we made there was a nod from below from the slumbering helmsman. The waves, too, were sleepy, and across the wide trance of the sea, east nodded to west, and the sun was over all.

Suddenly bubbles seemed bursting beneath my closed eyes, and with a shock, I came back to life. And lo! Not forty fathoms off, a gigantic sperm whale lay rolling in the water like a large ship upside down, his broad glossy back glistening in the rays like a mirror! Lying lazily in the sea and spouting his jet, the whale looked like a man smoking his pipe on a warm afternoon. But that pipe, poor whale, was thy last. The sleepy ship and every sleeper in it all at once started into wakefulness, and more than a score of voices from all parts of the vessel shouted forth as the great fish slowly and regularly spouted the sparkling brine into the air.

"Clear away the boats!" cried Ahab. And obeying his own order, he dashed the helm down before the helmsman could handle the spokes. The sudden shouts of the crew must have alarmed the whale; and before the boats were down, he started to swim away. Ahab gave orders that not an oar should be used, and all must speak in whispers. So seated like Ontario Indians on the gunwales of the boats, we swiftly but silently paddled along. Finally, as we glided along in the chase, the whale flitted his tail forty feet into the air and then sank out of sight like a tower swallowed up.

"There go flukes!" [1] was the cry, an announcement immediately followed by Stubb's producing his match and lighting his pipe, for now there would be a rest. After a while the whale rose again, and being now in advance of the smoker's boat and much nearer to it than any of the others, Stubb counted upon the honor of the capture. It was known now that the whale had heard his attackers, and there was no longer any need to be silent. Paddles were dropped, and oars came loudly into play. And still puffing at his pipe, Stubb cheered his crew to the fight.

---

[1] The whale is going underneath the water.

A mighty change had come over the fish, and he was aware that he was in danger. "Start her, start the boat, my men! Don't hurry yourselves; take plenty of time, but start her; start her like thunderclaps, that's all!" cried Stubb, spluttering out the smoke as he spoke. "Start her, now; give 'em the long and strong stroke, Tashtego. Start her, Tash, my boy—start her, all; but keep cool, keep cool. Easy, easy, only start her like grim death and grinning devils, and raise the dead out of their graves, boys—that's all. Start her!"

"Woo-hoo! Wa-hee!" cried Tashtego in reply, raising some old war whoop to the skies, as every oarsman in the boat bounced forward with one tremendous stroke.

But his wild screams were answered by others quite as wild. "Kee-hee! Kee-hee!" yelled Daggoo, straining forward and backward on his seat.

"Ka-la Koo-loo!" howled Queequeg, as if smacking his lips over a mouthful of steak. And thus with oars and yells, the boats cut the sea.

Meanwhile, Stubb, keeping his place at the head of the boats, still encouraged his men, all the while puffing the smoke from his mouth. Like desperadoes, they tugged and they strained until the welcome cry was heard—"Stand up, Tashtego! Give it to him!" The harpoon was hurled. The same moment something went hot and hissing along every oarsman's wrist. It was the magical line on the harpoon. As the line passed round and round the loggerhead,[2] it blisteringly passed through and through both of Stubb's hands, from which the handcloths, or squares of quilted canvas sometimes worn at these times, had accidentally dropped. It was like holding an enemy's sharp two-edged sword by the blade, and that enemy all the time striving to wrest it out of your clutch.

"Wet the line! Wet the line!" cried Stubb to one of the oarsmen, who snatched off his hat and dashed water into it. More turns were taken, so that the line began holding its place. The boat now flew through the water like a shark which was all fins. Thus they rushed,

---

[2] A round piece of timber around which the line is turned to keep it from going out too fast.

each man with might and main clinging to his seat to prevent being tossed to the foam. Whole Atlantics and Pacifics seemed passed as they shot on their way, until at length the whale slowed down in his flight.

"Haul in—haul in!" cried Stubb to the bowsman. And facing round toward the whale, all hands began pulling the boat up to him while yet the boat was being towed on. Soon ranging up by the side of the whale, Stubb, firmly planting his knee in the clumsy seat, sent dart after dart into the fish. At the word of command the boat would dodge from the angry whale, and then would range up again for another fling at him.

The red blood now poured from all sides of the monster like brooks down a hill. His tormented body rolled not in brine, but in blood, which bubbled and seethed. The slanting sun playing upon this crimson pond in the sea sent back its reflection in every face, so that they all glowed to each other like red men. And all the while jet after jet of white smoke shot from the whale, as it did from Stubb, as again and again the lance was sent into the whale.

"Pull up—pull up!" he now cried to the bowsman as the tired whale showed further signs of weakening. "Pull up! Close to!" and the boat ranged along the fish's side. Then reaching far over the bow, Stubb slowly churned his sharp lance into the fish and kept it there, carefully churning and churning, as if seeking to feel after some gold watch that the whale might have swallowed and which he were fearful of breaking before he could hook it out. But the gold watch he sought was the innermost life of the fish. And now it is struck; for, going into his "flurry," [3] the monster horribly wallowed in his blood,

[3] The jerking of a dying whale.

overwrapped himself in mad boiling spray, and the boat dodged away from the danger.

And now slowing down, the whale once more rolled out into view, surging from side to side. At last, gush after gush of clotted red gore, as if it had been red wine, shot into the air, and falling back again, it ran dripping down his motionless sides into the sea. His heart had burst.

"He's dead, Mr. Stubb," said Daggoo.

"Yes; both pipes smoked out!" And withdrawing his own pipe from his mouth, Stubb scattered the dead ashes over the water, and for a moment stood thoughtfully watching the vast corpse he had made.

Stubb's whale had been killed some distance from the ship; and using the three boats, we commenced the slow business of towing the whale to the *Pequod*. And now as we eighteen men with thirty-six arms and one hundred and eighty thumbs and fingers slowly toiled hour after hour at that sluggish corpse in the sea, it seemed hardly to budge at all, except at long intervals. Thus one can easily understand just how large a mass we had captured.

Darkness came on, but three lights up and down in the *Pequod*'s main rigging dimly guided our way. As we drew nearer, we saw Ahab dropping one of several more lanterns over the bulwarks. Looking over the whale for a moment, Ahab issued the usual orders for securing it for the night; and then handing his lantern to a seaman, he went into his cabin and did not come forward again until morning. Although the whale was dead, Ahab still seemed dissatisfied. Moby Dick was yet to be slain; and though a thousand other whales were brought to his ship, he would still not be satisfied until he had killed the white whale.

Very soon you would have thought from the sound on the *Pequod's* decks that all hands were preparing to cast the anchor in the deep, for heavy chains are being dragged along the deck and thrust rattling out of portholes. But by these clanking links, the vast corpse is to be tied to the ship. Tied by the head to the stern, and by the tail to the bows, the whale now lies with its black hull close to the vessel's.

Although Ahab was very quiet about it all, at least as far as could be known on deck, Stubb, his second mate, showed good-natured excitement. Such a bustle was he in, that Starbuck, his superior, turned over to him the sole management of affairs. One small, helping cause of all this liveliness was soon made known. Stubb was a high liver, and he was very fond of certain parts of the whale.

"A steak, a steak, before I sleep! You, Daggoo! Overboard you go and cut me one!" Although whalers do not as a general rule eat whale meat, yet now and then you find some of these Nantucketers who have a genuine relish for that particular part of the sperm whale which Stubb called for. About midnight the steak was cut and cooked; and lighted up by two lanterns of sperm oil, Stubb stoutly stood up to his supper. Nor was Stubb the only banqueter on whale's flesh that night. Thousands and thousands of sharks swarmed around the dead whale and feasted on its fatness. The few sleepers below in their bunks were often startled by the sharp slapping of shark tails against the hulls, within a few inches of the sleepers' hearts.

Peering over the side, you could just see them (as before you heard them) wallowing in the sullen, black waters and turning over on their backs as they scooped out huge pieces of the whale as large as a human head.

This particular feat of the shark seems almost unbelievable. How, at such a tough surface, they manage to gouge out such mouthfuls remains a mystery. The mark they leave on the whale is like the hollow made by a carpenter when he prepares the wood for a screw.

Sharks will be seen longingly gazing up to the ship's decks, like hungry dogs around a table where red meat is being carved, ready to grab every killed man that is tossed to them. There is no time or occasion when you will find sharks in such countless numbers and in gayer and more jovial spirits than around a dead sperm whale tied by night to a whale ship at sea. But, as yet, Stubb paid no attenton to the sharks snapping at the whale, no more than the sharks paid any attention to him.

"Cook, cook!" he cried, widening his legs still farther, as if to form a more secure base for his supper, and at the same time darting his fork into the dish, as if stabbing with his lance. "Cook, you cook! Sail this way, cook!"

"Cook," said Stubb, rapidly lifting a red bite to his mouth, "don't you think this steak is rather overdone? You've been beating this steak too much; it's too tender. Don't I always say that to be good a whale steak must be tough? There are those sharks now over the side. Don't you see they prefer it tough and rare? What a shindy they are kicking up! Cook, go and talk to 'em. Tell 'em they are welcome to help themselves, but they must keep quiet. Blast me, if I can hear my voice. Away, cook, and deliver my message. Here, take this lantern," snatching one from his sideboard. "Now then, go and preach to them!"

"But wait then, cook. You see this whale steak of yours was so very bad that I have put it out of sight as soon as possible. Well, for the future, when you cook another whale steak for me, I'll tell you what to do so as not to spoil it by overdoing. Hold the steak in one hand, and place a live coal to it with the other. When that is done, you may serve it, d'ye hear? And now tomorrow, cook, when we are cutting the fish, be sure you stand by to get the tips of his fins. Pickle them away for me. There, now you may go."

The fact is that among his hunters, at least, the whale would by all hands be considered a noble dish were there not so much of him. But when you come to sit down before a meat pie nearly one hundred feet long, it takes away your appetite.

But what further keeps the whale from being a dish for men is his richness. He is the great prize ox of the sea, too fat to be very good. Look at his hump, which would be as fine eating as the buffalo's were it not solid fat. Nevertheless, many whalemen have a method of using it with other food. In the long watches of the night, it is a common thing for the seamen to dip their ship biscuit into the huge oil pots and let them fry there awhile. Many a good supper have I thus made.

In the case of a small sperm whale, the brains are a fine dish. The casket of the skull is broken with an ax, the brains are drawn out and are then mixed with flour and cooked.

21 *We Become Butchers*

When, in the Southern Fishery, a captured sperm whale, after long and weary toil, is brought to the ship late at night, it is usually not customary to begin at once the business of cutting him to pieces. That business is a very hard one, is not very soon completed, and requires all hands in the job. Thus, the custom is to take in all sail, tie the helm, and then send everyone below to his hammock until daylight, with anchor watches being kept on the deck to see that all goes well.

But sometimes this plan will not work at all, because hosts of sharks sometimes gather around the dead whale, and were he left for six hours, say, on a stretch, little more than the skeleton would be seen by morning. In most parts of the ocean, however, sharks do not live in such large numbers, and they can be driven away from the dead whale by the use of sharp whaling spades. However, in some cases the stirring up of the sharks with the whaling spades has been known to cause them to attack the whale even more. It did not happen this way with the *Pequod*'s sharks, though, to be sure, any man not used to such sights who looked over her side that night would have almost thought the whole round sea was one huge cheese, and those sharks the maggots in it.

To protect our whale, a cutting stage was hung

over the side, three lanterns were lowered, and Quee-queg and another seaman, mounting the platform, darted their long whaling spades and heaped continual murder on the sharks. But in the foamy sea, it was not always possible to hit the mark. The sharks snapped viciously, not only at each other, but they also some-times bit themselves. Killed and hoisted on deck for the sake of his skin, one of these sharks almost took poor Queequeg's hand off when he tried to shut down the dead lid of his murderous jaw.

It was a Saturday night, and what a Sunday fol-lowed! The ivory *Pequod* was turned into what seemed a shamble, and every sailor was a butcher. You would have thought we were offering up ten thousand red oxen to the sea gods. And now, from over the side Star-buck and Stubb, the mates, armed with their long spades, began cutting a hole in the body of the whale for the in-sertion of a hook just above the nearest of the two side fins. This done, the hook is inserted, and the main body of the crew, striking up a wild chorus, now commences heaving in one dense crowd at the windlass. More and more the ship leans over to the whale, while every heave of the windlass is answered by a helping heave from the billows.[1] At last, a swift, startling snap is heard. With a great swash the ship rolls upwards and backwards from the whale, and the tackle rises into sight dragging after it the first strip of blubber.

In the business of cutting and attending to a whale, there is much running backwards and forwards among the crew. Now hands are wanted here, and then again hands are wanted there. There is no staying in any one place, for at one and the same time everything has to

[1] The surges, swells, or waves of the sea.

be done everywhere. It was mentioned that upon first breaking ground in the whale's back, the blubber hook was inserted into the original hole cut by the spades of the mates. But how did so clumsy and weighty a mass as that same hook get fixed in that hole? It was put there by my particular friend Queequeg, whose duty it was, as a harpooneer, to mount the monster's back for that special purpose.

It was necessary for Queequeg to stay on the whale until all of the stripping was done. So down there, some ten feet below the level of the deck, the poor harpooneer stays, half on the whale and half in the water. It was my duty to protect Queequeg with a rope, one end attached to him and the other to me. It was dangerous business for both of us, and should Queequeg sink to rise no more, then honor demanded that I should be dragged down, too. But though I handled the rope as carefully as I could, sometimes Queequeg jerked it so that I came very near sliding overboard. Nor could I forget that, do what I would, I had control of only one end of the rope.

I would often jerk poor Queequeg from between the whale and the ship, where he would occasionally fall, but this was not the only danger to which he was exposed. Forgetting the sharp spades used on them during the night, the sharks swarmed round the dead whale like bees in a beehive. And right in among these sharks was Queequeg, who often pushed them aside with his feet. It is a fact that sharks attacking a dead whale will seldom touch a man.

Besides the rope, with which I now and then jerked Queequeg from the mouth of a shark, he was provided with still another protection. Hanging over the side on a small platform, Tashtego and Daggoo swung over his head two keen whale spades, with which they slaughtered as many sharks as they could reach. They meant Queequeg's best happiness, I am certain, but in their attempts to keep the sharks away, they came dangerously near Queequeg. But poor Queequeg, I suppose, straining and gasping with that great iron hook, only prayed to his Yojo.

But courage! There is good cheer in store for you, Queequeg. For now, with blue lips and bloodshot eyes, the tired savage climbs the chains and stands all dripping and trembling over the side. The steward then hands him a cup of rum.

Now as the blubber envelops the whale exactly as the rind does an orange, so is it stripped from the body exactly as an orange is sometimes stripped. The strain kept up by the windlass continually keeps the whale rolling over and over in the water, and the blubber peels off and is cut into large hunks by Starbuck and Stubb. Then, piece by piece, it is all the time being hoisted higher and higher until the upper end grazes the maintop. The men at the windlass then cease heaving, and for a moment or two the blood-dripping mass sways to and fro, and every one present must be careful to dodge it when it swings, else it may box his ears and pitch him headlong overboard.

One of the harpooneers now advances with a long, keen weapon called a boarding sword, and watching his chance, he slices out a considerable hole in the lower part of the swaying mass. Into this hole a second tackle is then hooked so as to retain a hold upon the blubber in order to prepare for what follows. Then the harpooneer, warning all hands to stand off, makes a dash at the mass, and with a few sidelong slices, cuts it completely in two. This while the short lower part is still fast, the long upper strip, called a blanket piece, swings clear and is all ready for lowering. The heavers forward now resume their song, and while one tackle is peeling and hoisting a second strip from the whale, the other is slowly slackening away, and down goes the first strip through the main hatchway into an unfurnished parlor called the blubber room. And thus the work goes on, the two tackles hoisting and lowering at the same time, the whale and windlass heaving, the heavers singing, and the ship straining.

A word or two more concerning this matter of the skin or blubber of the whale. It has already been said that it is stripped from him in long pieces called blanket pieces. For the whale indeed is wrapped up in his blubber as in a real blanket. It is by reason of this cozy blanketing of his body that the whale can keep himself comfortable in all weathers, in all seas, times, and tides. What would become of a Greenland whale, say, in those shuddering icy seas of the north if he did not have his blanket? A whale, unlike most of the other cold water fish, like a man has lungs and warm blood. Freeze his blood and he dies.

"Haul in the chains! Let the carcass [2] go astern!" The vast tackles now have done their duties, and the peeled white body of the beheaded whale flashes like marble. Though it has changed in color, it still looks as large as ever. Slowly it floats more and more away, the water round it torn and splashed by sharks and the air above full of screaming birds whose beaks are like so many daggers in the whale. The vast white bulk floats

[2] Body.

further and further from the ship, and every rod that it floats the sharks and birds keep up their murderous work.

It should not have been omitted that just before the complete stripping of the dead whale, his head is cut off. The whale has nothing that can properly be called a neck, since his head and body seem to join in the thickest part of him. The man must cut off the head from above, some eight or ten feet between himself and the whale, and must work with the whale almost hidden in the sea. And at the same time, he has to cut many feet deep in the flesh, and he must know exactly where to cut because of bony structures. In spite of this Stubb boasted he needed but ten minutes to behead a sperm whale.

When first severed, the head is dropped back into the water and held there by a cable until the body is stripped. If the head belongs to a small whale, it is brought on deck and disposed of at once. But with a full-grown whale, this is impossible, for the sperm whale's head is nearly one-third of his entire bulk. The Pequod's whale being beheaded and the body stripped, the head was brought against the ship's side, about halfway out of the sea. There the head remained for some time, because there were other duties for the present.

The Pequod moved on, and soon the man on the mainmast head sighted another whaler which proved to be the Jeroboam, also from Nantucket. Ships of the American Whale Fleet have private signals which are collected in a book, a copy of which is carried by every captain. Thus the whale commanders can recognize each other on the ocean, even at long distances. As the two ships came close together, Starbuck prepared the ladder for the visiting captain, but the *Jeroboam*'s captain motioned that he was not coming aboard. It turned out that the *Jeroboam*'s crew had a contagious disease on board, and did not wish to expose any members of the *Pequod*'s crew. But it was possible for the two crews to talk, even though the sea was rough.

"I fear not thy disease, man," said Ahab from the bulwarks to the *Jeroboam*'s captain, who stood in the boat that had come fairly close. "Hast thou seen the white whale?" Then the *Jeroboam*'s captain began a dark story about Moby Dick.

After the ship had been out from Nantucket for more than a year, Moby Dick was sighted; and the chief mate, in spite of warnings about the ferocity of the beast, desired to try to bring him in. Five men were persuaded to help the mate, and they finally were able to fasten one iron in the beast.

Then a broad white shadow rose from the sea, and the next instant the mate was thrown into the air and fell into the sea a distance of fifty yards from the boat. Not a chip of the boat was harmed, nor were any of the other oarsmen, but the mate sank forever. Frightened, the crew of the boat gave up the chase.

Now, said the stranger captain to Ahab, did he still intend to hunt Moby Dick? "Aye," was Ahab's answer.

We still have a sperm whale's huge head hanging to the *Pequod*'s side, but we must continue to let it hang there awhile until we can get a chance to attend to it. For the present there are other things to do, and the best we can do now for the head is to pray that the tackles may hold.

During the past night and forenoon, the *Pequod* had gradually drifted into a sea where patches of yellow brit gave signs of right whales. Though the *Pequod* usually did not hunt this type of whale at all, because it was not so valuable as the sperm whale, to the surprise of all an announcement was made that a right whale should be captured that day if one could be found.

Soon tall spouts were seen, and two boats, Stubb's and Flask's, were sent in pursuit. Pulling further and further away, they at last became almost invisible. But suddenly in the distance, the men on the masthead saw a great heap of stirring white water, and soon after, the news came from the masthead that one or both of the boats must be attached to a whale.

A short time passed, and soon the boats were in plain sight, in the act of being dragged towards the ship by the whale. So close did the monster come to the ship that he seemed purposely to be trying to ram it, but he suddenly dived down under water. "Cut, cut!" was the cry from the ship to the boats, which, for one instant, seemed on the point of being brought with a deadly dash against the vessel's sides. But having plenty of line yet in the tubs and the whale not going down very fast, they let out an abundance of rope, and at the same time pulled with all their might so as to get ahead of the ship. For a few minutes the struggle was especially dangerous, and the boats seemed likely to be drawn under.

But the tired whale had slowed his speed, and changing his course, he went around the back of the ship, towing the two boats after him. And thus round and round the *Pequod* the battle went, while the sharks that had before swum around the sperm whale's body now rushed to the fresh blood that was spilled, thirstily drinking at every new gash. At last the whale's spout grew thick, and with a frightful roll and vomit, he turned upon his back a corpse.

"I wonder what the old man wants with this lump of foul lard," said Stubb not very pleasantly.

"Wants with it?" replied Flask. "Did you never hear that a ship which has a sperm whale head on one side and a right whale's on the other, can never turn over?"

"Why not?"

"I don't know, but I heard Fedallah say so, and he seems to know all about ship's charms. But I sometimes think he'll charm the ship to no good at last. I don't half like that chap, Stubb."

"Sink him!" said Stubb. "I never look at him at all.

But if I ever get a chance of a dark night, with Fedallah standing close by the bulwarks—." Stubb made a motion with both hands, and this indicated he would push Fedallah into the sea if the chance presented itself. "He's the devil, I say. Why does the old man have so much to do with him?" Stubb added.

"Striking up a swap or a bargain, I suppose," said Flask.

"Bargain? What about?"

"Why, do ye see, the old man is hard bent after the white whale, and the devil there is trying to come round him and get him to swap away his silver watch, or his soul, or something of the sort, and then he'll surrender Moby Dick."

"Pooh! Stubb, how can Fedallah do that?"

"I don't know, Flask, but the devil is a curious chap, and a wicked one, I tell ye. Well, then, pull ahead, and let's get this whale alongside."

The boats towed the whale on the left side of the ship, where chains and other necessities were already prepared for tying him there.

"Didn't I tell you so?" said Flask. "Yes, you'll soon see this right whale's head opposite the sperm whale's."

In good time, Flask's saying proved true. As before the Pequod leaned over toward the sperm whale's head. Now, with both heads, she rode even.

22   *Queequeg Goes to the Rescue*

As the ship sped on, the final work on the sperm whale, that of taking the treasure from his head, was begun. The sac in a large whale's head generally yields about five hundred gallons of sperm oil, though much of it spills, leaks, or dribbles away in the business of collecting it. When cutting off the head of a sperm whale, the cutter must be very careful or he will puncture the sac that holds the valuable sperm.

Tashtego climbs on top of the whale's head; and using a short-handled spade, he searches for the proper place to break into the tun, or sac, which holds the valuable sperm. He works very carefully, like a treasure hunter in some old house, sounding the walls to find where the gold is hidden. By the time his search is over, a stout, iron-bound bucket, just like a well bucket, to which a rope is attached, is handed him. Inserting a pole into the bucket, Tashtego downward guides the bucket into the sac until it entirely disappears. Then he gives the word to the seamen above, and they pull on the rope. Up comes the bucket bubbling like a dairymaid's pail of new milk. The vessel is caught and then quickly emptied into a large tub. This goes on through the same round until the cistern will yield no more. Toward the end, Tashtego has to ram his pole harder and harder and deeper and deeper into the sac until some twenty feet of the pole has gone down.

Now, the sailors of the *Pequod* had been bailing some time in this way. Several tubs had been filled with the valuable sperm, when all at once a queer accident happened. How it happened there is no telling now, but on a sudden, as the eightieth or ninetieth bucket came suckling up, poor Tashtego dropped head first down into the tun in the whale's head, and with a horrible oily gurgling went clean out of sight.

"Man overboard!" cried Daggoo, who amid the general excitement was the first to come to his senses. "Swing the bucket this way!" And putting one foot into it, he was hoisted to the top of the whale's head almost before Tashtego could have reached the bottom. Looking over the side, the men saw the dead whale's head throbbing and heaving just below the surface of the sea. Although it seemed that the dead whale's head had come to life, it was poor Tashtego struggling for life.

At this point a sharp, cracking noise was heard, and to the horror of all, one of the two enormous hooks holding the head tore out, and the head swung sideways. The ship reeled and shook as if hit by an iceberg. The one remaining hook, upon which the entire weight was now thrown, seemed every instant to be on the point of giving way.

"Come down, come down!" yelled the seamen to Daggoo, who rammed down the bucket into the sac, meaning that the harpooneer should grasp it and so be hoisted out.

"In heaven's name, man," cried Stubb. "How will that help him, jamming that iron-bound bucket on top of his head? Stop, will ye!"

"Stand clear of the tackle!" cried a voice like the bursting of a rocket. Almost at the same instant, with a thunderboom, the enormous mass dropped into the sea. Daggoo, through a thick mist of spray, was seen clinging to the tackles, while poor, buried-alive Tashtego was sinking down to the bottom of the sea. But hardly had the blinding vapor cleared away when a naked figure, with a sword in his hand, was for one swift moment seen hovering over the bulwarks. The next moment a loud splash announced that my brave Queequeg had dived to the rescue. One packed rush was made to the side, and every eye counted every ripple, as moment fol-

lowed moment, and no sign of either the sinker or diver could be seen. Some hands now jumped into a boat alongside and pushed a little off from the ship.

"Ha! Ha!" cried Daggoo all at once from his now quiet swinging perch overhead. And looking far off from the side, we saw an arm thrust upright from the blue waves, a sight strange to see, as an arm thrust from the grass over a grave.

"Both! Both! It is both," cried Daggoo again with a joyful shout. And soon Queequeg was seen boldly striking out with one hand, and with the other clutching the long hair of Tashtego. Drawn into the waiting boat, they were quickly brought to the deck, but Tashtego was long in coming to, and Queequeg did not look very brisk.

Now, how had this noble rescue been done? Diving after the slowly descending head, Queequeg, with his keen sword, had made side lunges near its bottom and had made a large hole there. Then dropping his sword, he had thrust his long arm far inward and upward, and so hauled out poor Tash by the head.

23 We Race for a Whale

In due time we met the ship *Jungfrau* of Bremen, the master of which was Derick De Deer. At one time the greatest whaling people in the world, the Dutch and Germans are now among the least, but here and there, you still occasionally meet with their flag in the Pacific. For some reason, the *Jungfrau* seemed quite eager to talk to us. While yet some distance from the *Pequod*, she dropped a boat and her captain came toward us.

"What has he in his hand there?" cried Starbuck, pointing to something held by the German. "Impossible! —a lamp!"

"Not that," said Stubb. "No, no, it's a coffee pot, Mr. Starbuck; he's coming to make us some coffee."

"Go along with you," cried Flask. "It's a lamp and an oil can. He's out of oil, and has come a-begging."

However unusual it may seem for an oil ship to be borrowing oil on the whale ground, yet sometimes such a thing really happens, and Captain De Deer really did seek oil.

As the stranger captain mounted the deck, Ahab, not noticing the lamp in his hand, eagerly inquired of the white whale, but Derick soon told him, in broken English, that he knew nothing about Moby Dick. The visiting captain said his last drop of oil was gone, and that his ship had not been able to capture a single flying fish to supply his ship. Ahab then granted the visitor the oil that he needed.

After he had been given the oil, the captain departed, but he had not gained his ship's side when whales were sighted from the mastheads of both vessels. So eager for the chase was Captain De Deer that, without putting lamp and oil aboard his ship, he made after the whales. He and three other German boats that followed him were considerably ahead of the *Pequod*'s boats. The whales—there were eight of them—soon were aware of the danger, and, all abreast, like so many spans of horses, sped straight before the wind.

Many fathoms in the rear swam a huge, humped old bull, which went so slowly that he seemed to be sick. His spout was short and slow, coming forth with a choking sort of gush. The old whale heaved his aged bulk, exposing the loss of a fin on his right side. Whether he lost that fin in battle, or had been born without it, it would be hard to say.

"Only wait a bit, old chap, and I'll give ye a sling for that wounded arm!" cried cruel Flask, pointing to the whale line near him.

"Mind he don't sling thee with it," cried Starbuck. "Give way or the Germans will have him."

All of the rival boats were pointed for this one fish, not only because he was the largest and therefore the most valuable, but because he was nearest to them. The other whales had traveled at such speed that it was almost impossible to catch them, for the time being, at least. At this point the *Pequod*'s boats had passed the three German boats last lowered; but from the great start he had, the German captain's boat still led the chase, though the men of the *Pequod*'s boats were gaining on him every moment.

The only thing Ahab's men were afraid of was that Derick, who was already so close to the whale, would be able to dart his iron before they could overtake and pass him. As for Derick, he seemed quite confident that this would be the case, and occasionally he mockingly shook his lamp at the *Pequod*'s boats.

"The dog!" cried Starbuck. "He dares me with the very lamp I filled for him not five minutes ago." And then speaking to his oarsmen, he shouted, "Give way, greyhounds! Dog to it, and pull!"

"I tell ye what it is, men," cried Stubb to his crew. "It's against my religion to get mad, but are ye going to let him beat ye? Do ye love brandy? Pull, won't ye? A barrel of brandy to the best man. Come, why don't some of ye burst a blood vessel? Who's been dropping an anchor overboard? We don't budge an inch. Halloa, here's grass growing in the boat's bottom, and the mast there's budding. This won't do, boys."

"Oh! see the suds he makes!" shouted Flask, dancing up and down. "Oh! my lads, do pull. Slapjacks [1] for supper, you know, my lads, baked clams and muffins. Don't lose him now. There goes three thousand dollars, men! A bank, a whole bank! What's this German about now?"

"Pull now, men, like fifty thousand line-of-battleship loads of red-haired devils," cried Stubb. The *Pequod*'s three boats were almost abreast the German captain's craft, but the German had so decided a start that he still would have won the race had not his midship oarsman caught a crab.[2] While the oarsman tried to free his oar, Derick's boat almost turned over. This made it pos-

---

[1] Flapjacks, griddle cakes, or pancakes.
[2] Made a faulty stroke with his oar.

sible for Starbuck, Stubb, and Flask to catch up with the German boat, and all were just behind the whale.

It was a terrific and maddening sight. The whale was now going head out, and sending his spout before him, while his one poor fin beat his side in an agony of fright. So have I seen a bird with clipped wing making scared broken circles in the air, trying to escape from hawks. But the bird has a voice and will make known her fear, but the fear of this vast dumb brute of the sea was chained up in him. He had no voice save his spout.

Seeing now that but a very few moments more would give the *Pequod*'s boats the advantage, Derick decided to take a chance and throw an unusually long harpoon. But no sooner did his harpooneer stand up to throw the dart than Queequeg, Tashtego and Daggoo darted their harpoons over the head of the German harpooneer, and their three irons entered the whale. Blinding vapors and white fire! The *Pequod*'s three boats, now tied to the whale, bumped into the German's with such force that both Derick and his harpooneer spilled out and were sailed over by the three *Pequod* boats.

"Don't be afraid," shouted Stubb, glancing at them as he shot by. "Ye'll be picked up later, but I saw some sharks behind. Hurrah! this is the way to sail now." But the monster's run was a brief one. Giving a sudden gasp, he dived under the water. As the three boats lay there on that gently rolling sea, not a single groan or cry of any sort, not so much as a ripple or a bubble, came up from the depths. A short time later Derick and his boat crew were rescued.

"Stand by, men. He stirs," cried Starbuck, as the three lines suddenly moved in the water. The next moment, relieved in great part by the pull downward, the boats gave a sudden bounce upward, as a small icefield will when a sense herd of white bears are scared into the sea.

"Haul in, haul in!" cried Starbuck again. "He's rising." The lines, of which hardly an instant before not an inch could have been gained, were now in long quick coils flung back all dripping into the boats, and soon the whale broke water within two ship lengths of the hunters. The whale's motions showed he was tired. In most land animals there are certain valves or floodgates in many of their veins, and when these animals are wounded, the blood is in some degree shut off in certain directions. Not so with the whale. When he is cut by even so small a point as a harpoon, a deadly drain is at once begun upon his system. Yet so vast is the amount of blood in him that he will keep bleeding and bleeding for a long time.

As the boats now more closely surrounded him, the whole upper part of his form, with much of it that is ordinarily under water, was plainly shown. His eyes, or rather the places where the eyes had been, were revealed. For all his old age, his one arm, and his blind eyes, he must die the death and be murdered to provide oil for the use of men. Still rolling in his blood, the whale showed a strangely discolored bump, the size of a bushel, low down on his flank.

"A nice spot," cried Flask. "Just let me stick him there once."

"Stop!" shouted Starbuck. "There's no need for that!"

But kind Starbuck was too late. At the instant of Flask's dart, a jet of liquid shot from the cruel wound, and the whale, now spouting thick blood, turned over

Flask's boat. But this was his death stroke. For by this time he was so spent by loss of blood that he helplessly rolled away from the wreck he had made. He lay panting on his side, flapped with his stumped fin, turned up the white secrets of his belly, lay like a log, and died. It was a piteous sight, that last spout.

Soon, while the crews were awaiting the arrival of the ship, the whale showed signs of sinking. Immediately, Starbuck ordered lines tied to it at different points so that every boat was a buoy.[1] When the ship drew near, the whale was transferred to her side, and was strongly tied there, for it was plain that if it were not tied securely, the body would at once sink to the bottom.

It so chanced that almost upon the first cutting into him with the spade, the entire length of a rusted harpoon was found imbedded in his flesh. But still more curious was the fact that a lance-head of stone was found in him not far from the buried iron, and the flesh was perfectly firm about it. Who had darted that stone lance and when? It might have been darted by some Northwest Indian long before America was discovered.

There might have been other marvels found in this old whale, there is no telling. But a sudden stop was put to further discoveries when the ship began to be dragged sideways to the sea, because of the whale's tendency to sink. However, Starbuck, who had charge of the whale, hung onto it to the last. When he finally did give the command to break clear from it, there was so much strain on the timberheads that it was impossible to cast off the chains and cables.

Meanwhile everything on the *Pequod* was aslant.

[1] A floating object used for marking a channel or obstruction.

To cross to the other side of the deck was like walking up the steep roof of a house. Further attempts, none of which was successful, were made to release the chains and cables, and every moment the ship seemed on the point of going over.

Then Queequeg, seizing the carpenter's heavy hatchet, leaned out of a porthole, and steel to iron, began slashing at the largest chains that held the whale. Only a few strokes, full of sparks, were given when the heavy pull on the chains did the rest. With a terrific snap, the ship righted itself, and the fish sank.

This occasional sinking of a recently killed sperm whale is a very curious thing, and no fisherman really knows what causes it. Usually the dead sperm whale floats easily, with its side or belly quite a bit above the surface of the water. If only the old whales sank, then you might think that age had something to do with it, but it is not so. For young whales, in the best of health, sometimes sink, too.

It was not long after the sinking of the body that a cry was heard from the *Pequod*'s mastheads announcing that the *Jungfrau* was again lowering her boats. However, the only spout in sight was that of a fin back whale, which can not be captured because it is such a fast swimmer. The fin back's spout is so like the sperm whale's that fishermen who are not skilled hunters often mistake the two.

24 We Find Pirates and the Great Whale Herd

For many ages the pirates of Malay, hiding among the low shaded coves and islets of Sumatra, have attacked the vassels sailing through these waters, fiercely demanding goods or money at the point of their spears. Though probably not so bold now as they once were, because certain European ships have at various times bloodily beaten them off, yet even at this present day we occasionally hear of English and American vessels in those waters which have been boarded and robbed.

With a fair, fresh wind, the *Pequod* was now drawing nigh to these waters. Ahab wished to pass through them into the Java Sea, to go northward over waters which sometimes contained the sperm whale, sweep inshore by the Philippine Islands, and then gain the far coast of Japan in time for the great whaling season there. This route would cause the *Pequod* to travel almost all the sperm whale cruising grounds of the world. Then Ahab would travel to the Line [1] in the Pacific, where he counted upon finding and giving battle to Moby Dick. Ahab had so planned his voyage so as to arrive at the Line at the time Moby Dick would most likely be in those waters.

But is it possible for the *Pequod* to make this long

[1] The equator.

trip without touching land anywhere? Surely Ahab will stop for water. Nay, Ahab will not stop, but will continue his determined search for the white whale. The world-wandering whale ship, carrying no cargo but her crew, their weapons, and their wants, carries her own provisions. She carries water in her to last for many years; and the whalers prefer Nantucket water, even though it has been carried for three years, to yesterday's water collected from Peruvian or Indian streams. Thus it is that while other ships may have gone from China to New York and back again, touching at a score of ports, the whale ship in the same distance may not have sighted one grain of soil, her crew having seen no man but floating seamen like themselves.

Many sperm whales had been captured on the western coast of Java, near the Straits of Sunda, and it was known to be an excellent spot for whaling. And as the *Pequod* came nearer and nearer to the place, the lookouts were told to keep wide awake. But for a long time we saw no whales, and had just about given up the idea of finding any game when a cry was heard from the lookout. We were soon to see something very unusual.

Because of the extensive hunting of the sperm whale over all oceans, the monsters quite often travel in large herds, although in former times they were usually found in small herds. It would seem that the whales had joined themselves together to protect themselves against the deadly harpoons. Thus you may now sometimes sail for weeks and months together without being greeted by a single spout, and then be suddenly saluted by what seems thousands and thousands of sperm whales.

This was what happened as we cruised through the narrow waters. On both sides of the ship, at a distance of two or three miles, and forming a great halfcircle, a continual chain of whale jets was playing and sparkling in the noonday air. The jets resembled some thousand cheerful chimneys of some large city on a cool autumn morning. This vast fleet of whales seemed to be hurrying forward through the straits as would an army approaching a mountain cut in unfriendly territory.

Crowding all sail, the *Pequod* pressed after them, the harpooneers handling their weapons and loudly

cheering from the heads of their hanging boats. If the wind only held, the harpooners had little doubt that they would capture some of the whales once they were out in open water. And who could tell, perhaps in the whale fleet Moby Dick himself might be swimming! So, with sail piled on sail, we sailed along, driving the herd before us. Suddenly the voice of Tashtego was heard loudly calling our attention to something behind us.

Leveling his glass at the sight, Ahab quickly revolved in his pivot hole and cried, "Set the sails to give the ship all the speed possible. The Malays are after us!" Ahab paced the deck, watching the whale herd he chased and the bloodthirsty pirates who were chasing him. But the speedy *Pequod* soon outdistanced the pirates, and shot out upon the broad waters beyond. But the harpooneers seemed more to grieve that the swift whales had been gaining upon the ship than to rejoice that the ship had left the pirates behind. Driving ahead after the whales at renewed speed, the ship once more was gaining, and the whales seemed to have slowed down somewhat. The word was passed to take to the boats.

No sooner were the boats down than the whales rallied again, and forming in close ranks, redoubled their speed. Stripped to our shirts, we sprang to our oars. But after several hours of pulling, we were almost ready to quit the chase when the whales became gallied.[2] The columns in which they had been swimming had been broken, and they all seemed to be going mad. In all directions and in vast irregular circles they were swimming, showing panic. Some of the whales seemed completely helpless and floated like empty ships

[2] To be frightened excessively.

on the sea. The herd now resembled a flock of sheep attacked by wolves.

This fear is common to all herding creatures, and is not limited to the whale. Though banding together in tens of thousands, the lion-maned buffaloes of the West have fled before a single horseman. Notice, too, how human beings, herded together in a theatre, crowd, trample, and jam each other to death at the slightest alarm of fire.

Though many of the whales were in violent motion, yet it is to be noticed that as a whole the herd neither advanced nor retreated, but remained in one place. As is customary in those cases, the boats at once separated and each made for some lone whale outside the herd. Our boat, having fastened on a fish, was plunged forward, and we tore a white gash in the sea. On all sides, as we flew by, were the crazed creatures rushing to and fro about us. We knew not at what moment we might be locked in and crushed.

But not a bit afraid, Queequeg steered us manfully, now dodging this monster directly across our route and now edging away from another one. Starbuck stood up in the bows, lance in hand, pricking out of our way whatever whales he could reach by short darts, for there was no time to make long ones.

All whaleboats carry devices called druggs, invented by Nantucket Indians. Two thick squares of wood of equal size are clenched together. A line of considerable length is then attached to the middle of this block. The other end of the line is looped so that it can in a moment be fastened to a harpoon. It is chiefly among gallied whales that the drugg is used. For then, more whales are close around you than you can possibly chase at one time. But sperm whales are not found every day; while you may, then, you must kill all you can. And if you can not kill them all at once, you must wing them so that they can afterward be killed at your leisure.

Our boat was furnished with three of them. The first and second were successfully darted, and we saw the whales staggeringly running off, dragging the heavy drugg. They were tied with what seemed a ball and chain. When we flung the third drugg, the clumsy wooden block caught under one of the seats of the boat, and in an instant tore it out and carried it away. The oarsman was dropped in the boat's bottom as the seat slid from under him. On both sides the sea came in from the damaged planks, but we stuffed two or three shirts in, and so stopped the leaks for the time.

At last the harpoon in the whale which was pulling us came out, and the whale vanished. We then glided between two whales into the heart of the herd, as if we had slid into some quiet mountain lake. Here the storms from the other whales were heard but not felt. In the distance we saw pods of whales, eight or ten in each, going round and round like spans of horses in a ring. Because there was such a crowd of whales around us, we saw no possible chance to escape at that time. We must watch for a break in the living wall that hemmed us in; the wall that had only admitted us in order to shut us up. Keeping at the center of the lake, we were sometimes visited by small tame cows and calves, the women and children of the herd.

The smaller whales, now and then visiting our boat, did not seem at all frightened. Like household dogs, they came snuffing round us, until it seemed almost as if they were tame. Queequeg patted their foreheads. Starbuck scratched their backs with his lance, but he did not dart it for he feared for the safety of the boat. Floating on their sides, the mothers seemed to be quietly watching us, and one of the little infants, which seemed to be hardly a day old, must have measured some fourteen feet in length and some six feet around.

While we were thus hemmed in, we could in the distance see the other boats drugging whales on the outside of the herd. But the sight of the angry drugged whales now and then blindly darting to and fro across the circles was nothing to what at last met our eyes. A whale had become entangled in a harpoon line that he pulled after him. He also had run away with the cutting spade in him. Tormented to madness, he was now churning through the water, tossing his tail, and swinging about him the keen spade, which had worked loose from his flesh. The spade was murdering and wounding his own comrades.

This terrific object seemed to recall the whole herd from their stationary fright, and the whales began to swim in thickening clusters. Yes, the long calm was departing. A low advancing hum was soon heard. And then, like a river breaking up in the spring, the entire host of whales came tumbling upon the inner circle where our boat was resting. Instantly Starbuck and Queequeg changed places, Starbuck taking the stern.

"Oars! Oars!" Starbuck whispered, seizing the helm, as the whales charged in. "Grip your oars! Shove him off, you, Queequeg—the whale there—prick him— hit him! Stand up, and stay so! Spring, men—pull, men. Never mind their backs—scrape them—scrape away!"

The boat was now all but jammed between two vast black bulks, leaving only a narrow channel. But by an unusual effort, we finally were able to escape the danger of being crushed by the two monsters. After other similar hair-breadth escapes, we at last swiftly glided into what had been one of the outer circles, which now was being crossed by whales. The whales, now having clumped together at last in one dense body, then continued their onward flight with great speed.

Further pursuit was useless. But the boats still lingered to pick up drugged whales that had not been able to flee and to secure one which Flask had killed. There is a saying in the whale fishery that the more whales there are the less fish, and this certainly proved true in our case. Of all the drugged whales, only one was captured. The rest managed to escape for the time, but only to be taken by some ship other than the *Pequod*.

It frequently happens that when several ships are hunting together, a whale may be struck by one vessel, then escape, and be finally killed or captured by another vessel. For example, after a weary and dangerous chase and capture of a whale, the body may get loose from the ship by reason of a violent storm. Then a second ship retakes the whale, and snugly tows it alongside without risk of life or line. Many violent disputes follow, as might be expected.

Although no nation has ever written any whaling law, American fishermen have been their own legislators and lawyers in this matter. Yet these laws might be engraved on the barb of a harpoon so short are they. There are only two parts to it: I. A Fast-Fish belongs to the party fast to it; II. A Loose-Fish is fair game for anybody who can soonest catch it. But these two laws are so brief that they need explaining.

First, what is a Fast-Fish? Alive or dead a fish is called fast when it is connected with a ship. In the same way, a fish is called fast when it bears anything showing ownership. But the party claiming a fish must show his ability and intention of taking the fish alongside. All other fish are considered Loose-Fish.

25 *The* Pequod *Meets the* Rosebud

A week or two after the last whaling scene told about, a strange, not very pleasant smell was noticed, although the men on the lookouts reported nothing in the distance.

"I will bet something now," said Stubb, "that somewhere near are some of those drugged whales we stuck the other day. I thought some of them would die before long." In due time in the distance was sighted a ship, whose furled sails indicated that some sort of whale must be alongside. As we came nearer, the vessel was flying a French flag; and because of the birds that were swooping around the ship, it was clear that the whale alongside must be what fishermen call a blasted whale. A blasted whale is a dead fish that has been found and taken alongside. It is easy to imagine what a foul smell such a large amount of dead fish meat would make. Yet there are some whaling ships that will take them, even though the oil obtained from such a fish is of very little value.

Coming nearer, we saw that the French ship had a second whale alongside, and this second whale was partly dried up. The *Pequod* had not swept so near to the stranger that Stubb said he recognized his cutting spade in the lines that were knotted around the tail of one of the whales. "That ship is content with what we have left," said Stubb. "I mean the drugged whale there. What oil he'll get from the drugged whale there wouldn't be fit to burn in a jail. And as for the other whale, now that I think of it, it may contain something worth a good deal more than oil—ambergris."

Ambergris, which is very valuable, is soft, waxy, and so highly fragrant that it is largely used for perfumes, precious candles, and hair dressing. Some wine merchants drop a few grains into fine wine to flavor it. Who would think, then, that such fine ladies and gentlemen should use something found in the bowels of a sick whale! Yet so it is.

Stubb guessed correctly that the strangers did not know that the dried up whale probably contained ambergris, and he decided he would try to bargain for the shrunken carcass. Calling his boat crew, he drew near the ship, which was called the *Rosebud.* "A wooden rosebud, eh?" he cried with his hands to his nose, "but how it smells! Are there any of you that speak English?"

"Yes," answered one of the men from the bulwarks, who turned out to be the chief mate.

"Well, then, my *Rosebud,* have you seen the white whale?"

"What whale?"

"The white whale—a sperm whale—Moby Dick, have ye seen him?"

"Never heard of such a whale."

"Very good, then. Goodbye now, and I'll call again in a minute." Then rapidly pulling back toward the *Pequod* and seeing Ahab leaning over the rail awaiting his report, Stubb shouted, "No, sir! They have not seen the white whale." Ahab then left and Stubb returned to the French ship.

"What's the matter with your nose, there?" said Stubb speaking to the chief mate who had slung his nose in a sort of a bag. "Broke it?"

"What are you holding yours for?" questioned the chief mate, who showed he didn't like the job he was doing.

"Oh, nothing," explained Stubb with a smile. "It's a wax nose. I have to hold it on. But joking aside, do you know it's all foolishness trying to get oil out of such whales? As for that dried up one there, he isn't worth anything."

"I know that well enough," said the chief mate, "but the captain here won't believe it. This is his first voyage. But come aboard, and maybe he'll believe you, if he won't me, and so I'll get out of this dirty scrape."

"Anything to please ye, my sweet and pleasant fellow," added Stubb, who was soon on the deck. Stubb soon saw that the *Rosebud* crew was looking for an excuse to throw the ill-smelling whales overboard; he also found that they knew nothing about ambergris. However, since the *Rosebud* captain was still determined to use the whales, Stubb, with the chief mate acting as interpreter, decided to play a trick on him. The chief mate, since he was the only one aboard who could speak English, was to tell the captain whatever he wished, but he was to pretend he was speaking for Stubb.

"He says, captain," said the chief mate, "that only yesterday his ship saw a vessel whose captain and chief mate, with six sailors, had all died of fever caught from a blasted whale they had brought alongside." The captain looked worried, and the chief mate continued, "Our visitor says that the dried up whale is far more deadly than the blasted one. And if we value our lives, we should cut loose from these fish."

At once the captain ran forward, and ordered the whales dropped into the sea. By this time, Stubb was over the side, and pretending to help the *Rosebud* get

away from the dead fish, he threw his towline over the dried up one. Of course, this was the whale he wanted for himself. Presently a breeze sprang up, and Stubb acted as if he intended to cast the whale off his towline, but you may be sure that he did not. Soon the French ship was some distance away.

Then Stubb quickly pulled on the floating body, and told his fellow sailors on the *Pequod* of his trick. Seizing his sharp boat spade, he commenced digging into the body of the dried up whale, a little beyond the side fin. You would almost have thought he was digging a cellar there in the sea. His boat's crew were all in high excitement, eagerly helping their chief, and looking as anxious as gold hunters. All the time numberless fowls were diving, ducking, screaming, yelling, and fighting around them.

Stubb was beginning to look disappointed when suddenly from out of the whale there was a smell like perfume. "I have it, I have it!" cried Stubb. Dropping his spade, he put both hands in and drew out handfuls of something that looked like soap or old cheese. You might easily dent it with your thumb; it is of a hue between yellow and ash color. And this, good friends, is ambergris, worth a gold guinea [1] an ounce to any druggist. Some six handfuls were obtained, but more was lost in the sea. Still more might have been obtained had not Ahab at this time ordered Stubb to come on board.

A few days after the ambergris was obtained, one of Stubb's oarsmen strained his hand, and a boy named Pip was put in his place. Pip, who had come from Connecticut, had not had much experience at whaling. Upon the second lowering, the boat paddled upon the whale, and the fish received the darted iron. It gave its usual rap, which happened in this instance to be right under poor Pip's seat. Frightened, Pip jumped from the boat into the sea and became tangled in the whale line, and almost at the same instant the stricken whale started on a fierce run; Pip was in great danger of being choked to death.

To cut the rope was the only thing to do, but the whale was lost. Stubb, who was very angry, said to Pip, "Stick to the boat, Pip, or I won't pick you up if you jump. Bear that in mind and don't jump any more." But Pip jumped again, and when the whale started to run, Pip was left behind in the sea. Stubb really did not intend to leave Pip to drown. He thought the two boats in the rear would see him and pick him up. But it so happened that those boats, without seeing Pip, spied whales, turned, and gave chase. By chance, the ship rescued him, but the terrible experience caused Pip to lose his mind.

[1] An English coin, no longer used, which was worth approximately $5.

26   *Ahab Meets the Captain with the Ivory Arm*

"Ship, ahoy! Hast seen the white whale?" So cried Ahab, calling to an English ship. With trumpet to his mouth, the old man was standing in his quarter-boat, his ivory leg plainly showing to the stranger captain. The stranger was a darkly tanned, strong, good-natured, fine-looking man of about sixty, and one empty arm of his jacket showed.

"Hast seen the white whale?" shouted Ahab again.

"See you this?" answered the stranger, who then showed a white arm of sperm whale bone which ended in a wooden head like a hammer.

"Man my boat!" cried Ahab, tossing the oars about him. In less than a minute, he and his crew were dropped to the water and were soon alongside the stranger. But a problem presented itself. In the excitement of the moment Ahab had forgotten that since the loss of his leg, he had never once stepped on board any vessel at sea except his own. The *Pequod,* as has been explained, was especially equipped to make it easy for him, but, of course, no other ship could be so changed at a moment's warning. Now it is no very easy matter for anybody—except for those who are almost hourly used to it, like whalemen—to climb up a ship's side from a boat on the open sea. Thus, Ahab could hardly hope to make the height at all.

As good luck would have it, the English ship had had a whale alongside a day or two before, and the great tackles were still there, the blubber hook still attached to one end. This was quickly lowered to Ahab, who slipped his one good leg through the hook (it was like sitting in the fork of an apple tree), and then giving the word, he was soon gently landed inside the bulwarks. With his ivory arm frankly thrust forth in welcome, the other captain advanced, and Ahab, putting out his ivory leg and crossing the ivory arm like two swordfish blades, cried out, "Let us shake bones together! An arm and a leg! An arm that never can shrink, d'ye see, and a leg that never can run. Where didst thou see the white whale and how long ago?"

"The white whale?" questioned the Englishman, pointing his ivory arm toward the east and taking a sad sight along it as if it had been a telescope. "I saw him on the Line last season."

"And he took that arm off, did he?" asked Ahab, now resting on the Englishman's shoulder.

"Yes, he was the cause of it. And your leg, too?"

"Spin me the yarn," said Ahab. "How was it?"

"It was the first time in my life I ever cruised on the Line," began the Englishman. "I did not know about the white whale at the time. Well, one day we lowered for a pod of four or five whales, and my boat fastened to one of them. A regular circus horse he was, too, since he ran in circles. All at once up from the bottom of the sea came a bouncing great whale, with a milky-white head and hump, all wrinkles."

"It was Moby Dick, it was he!" shouted Ahab, letting out his breath.

"And harpoons were sticking in his right side," continued the English captain.

"They were mine, my irons!" cried Ahab. "But go on!"

"Give me a chance, then," said the Englishman, with good nature. "Well, this old great-grandfather, with the white head and hump, runs into the pod and snaps furiously at my fast-line."

"Yes, I see! He wanted to free the fish that was caught. I know him."

"How it was exactly," continued the one-armed commander, "I do not know, but in biting the line, the white whale caught it in his teeth; so when we afterwards pulled on the line, we came plump onto his hump instead of the other whales! Seeing how matters stood and what a noble whale it was—the noblest and biggest I ever saw—I tried to capture him in spite of the boiling rage he seemed to be in. Thinking the line might come loose from his teeth, I snatched the first harpoon handy and let this old great-grandfather have it. But man alive! The next instant I was blind as a bat, both eyes out. The whale's tail went straight into the air like a marble steeple.

"As I was reaching for a second iron to toss into him, down comes his tail, cutting my boat in two and leaving each half in splinters. To escape his terrible beatings, I seized hold of my harpoon pole sticking in him, and for a moment clung to that. But the sea dashed me off, and at the same instant, the whale, taking one good dart forward, went down like a flash. As he did so, the barb of the second iron caught me here." The English captain placed his hand just below his shoulder.

"Yes," he continued, "caught me just here, I say, and started pulling me down to the bottom of the ocean. But all of a sudden, thank the good God, the barb ripped its way through the flesh, clear along the whole length of my arm, came out near my wrist, and up I floated. That gentleman there, Dr. Bunger, ship's surgeon, will tell you the rest. Now, Bunger boy, spin your part of the yarn."

The man who was pointed out had been all the time standing near them, but there was nothing about him to indicate that he was a surgeon. When he was introduced to Ahab, the surgeon bowed politely and began to tell of the accident, as he had been told to do. "It was a shocking bad wound," began the whale surgeon, "and taking my advice, the captain pointed the ship northward to get out of the blazing hot weather. But in spite of everything I could do, the wound kept getting worse and worse. The truth was, sir, it was as ugly a gaping wound as a surgeon ever saw—more than two feet and several inches long! In short the arm grew black; I knew what was threatened, and it was necessary for me to cut the limb off. But I had no part in making that ivory arm. That is the captain's work, not mine. He ordered the carpenter to make it."

"What became of the white whale?" demanded Ahab, who was not much interested in what the two men had to say except as their talk concerned Moby Dick.

"Oh," cried the one-armed captain, "oh, yes! Well, after he had gone down, we didn't see him again for some time. At that time I didn't then know what whale it was that had caused me to lose my arm. But sometime afterwards we heard about Moby Dick, and then I knew that it was he."

"Did you ever see him again?" questioned Ahab.

"Twice."

"But could not fasten your harpoons in him?"

"Didn't want to try to. Ain't the loss of one limb

enough? What should I do without this other arm? And I am thinking Moby Dick doesn't bite so much as he swallows. He's welcome to the arm he has since I can't help it and didn't know him then, but not to another one. No more white whales for me! I've lowered for him once, and that has satisfied me. There would be great glory in killing him, I know that, and there is a ship-load of precious sperm in him, but he's best left alone, don't you think so, Captain?" The English captain glanced at Ahab's ivory leg.

"He is," answered Ahab, "but I shall still hunt him. How long has it been since you last saw him? Which way was he heading?"

"Bless my soul," cried Dr. Bunger walking around Ahab. "This man's blood is at the boiling point. Bring the thermometer."

"Go away!" roared Ahab. "Which way was the whale heading?" He pushed the surgeon against the bulwarks. "Man the boat!"

"Good God!" cried the English captain, to whom the question was put. "What's the matter? He was heading east, I think. Is your captain crazy?" He whispered the last to Fedallah.

But Fedallah, putting a finger on his lip, slid over the bulwarks to take the boat's steering oar, and Ahab, swinging the cutting tackle toward him, commanded the ship's sailors to lower him. In a moment he was placed in the boat, and his men sprang to their oars. The English captain tried to stop him, but Ahab did not turn his head.

27 Ahab Follows Starbuck's Advice

As is customary, some members of the crew were pumping the ship one morning, but at this particular time there was much concern because a great deal of oil came up with the water. This meant that some of the casks below must have sprung bad leaks, and Starbuck went down into the cabin to report the matter to Ahab.

Now from the south and west, the *Pequod* was drawing near Formosa and the Bashee Isles, between which lies one of the outlets from the China waters into the Pacific. And so Starbuck found Ahab with a map of the area spread before him. With his snow-white ivory leg braced against the screwed leg of his table, and with a long pruning hook of a jackknife in his hand, the old man, with his back to the door, was wrinkling his brow and tracing his old courses again.

"Who's there?" growled Ahab, hearing the footstep at the door, but not turning round to it. "On deck! Begone!"

"Captain Ahab, it is I, Starbuck. The oil in the bottom of the ship is leaking, sir. We must up Burtons and break out." [1]

"Up Burtons and break out? Now that we are nearing Japan, do you expect me to stop for a week and tinker with a number of old barrels?"

---

[1] To bring the barrels to the top deck and examine them.

"Either do that, sir, or waste in one day more oil than we may make good in a year. What we came twenty thousand miles to get is worth saving, sir."

"So it is, so it is, if we get it."

"I was speaking of the oil in the hold, sir."

"And I was not speaking or thinking of that at all. Begone! Let it leak! Starbuck, I'll not have the Burtons hoisted!"

"What will the owners say, sir?"

"Let the owners stand on Nantucket beach and out-yell the winds. What cares Ahab? Owners, owners? Thou art always talking to me, Starbuck, about those greedy owners as if the owners were my conscience. But look ye, the only real owner of anything is its commander. On deck!"

"Captain Ahab," said the reddening mate, moving farther into the cabin.

"Devils! On deck!" shouted Ahab; and when Starbuck still did not obey, he seized a loaded musket from the rack and pointed it toward him. "There is one God that is Lord over the earth, and one captain that is lord over the *Pequod*—on deck!"

Starbuck moved in a calm manner, but as he left the cabin, he said, "I would not tell you to be afraid of me, although you have made me angry. That would only make you laugh. But beware of thyself, old man."

"He is brave, but he nevertheless obeys," murmured Ahab as Starbuck obeyed. "What's that he said—Ahab beware of Ahab—there's something there!" Then using the musket for a staff, he paced around in the little cabin. Finally he returned the gun to the rack and went on deck.

"Thou art too good a fellow, Starbuck," he said lowly to the mate, and then raising his voice to the crew added, "Up Burtons and break out in the mainhold!"

It would be hard to tell why Ahab finally decided to follow Starbuck's advice. It may have been a flash of honesty, or it may have been that Ahab wished to keep as much good feeling among the crew as he could. However it was, his orders were carried out, and the Burtons were hoisted.

It was found that the casks last placed into the hold were sound, and that the leak must be farther off. So, it being calm weather, they dug deeper and deeper into the barrels. Tierce [2] after tierce, too, of water, bread, and beef were hoisted out until at last they almost covered the entire upper deck. So top-heavy was the ship that it was well there were no storms then.

[2] A type of barrel.

28 *Queequeg Lies in His Coffin*

It was at this time that my poor pagan companion and close friend, Queequeg, was seized with a fever which almost took his life.

On a whaling boat, the higher you rise, until you get to be a captain, the harder you work. So it was with poor Queequeg, who, as a harpooneer, must not only face all the rage of the living whale, but, as we have elsewhere seen, must mount his dead back in a rolling sea. Finally, it was necessary that Queequeg descend into the hold, and bitterly sweating all day, move cask after cask to see whether any were leaking.

Poor Queequeg! When the ship was emptied of half of its casks from the hold, you could have seen him down in the bottom stripped to his woolen underwear. The tattooed savage crawling about amid that dampness and slime looked like a lizard at the bottom of a well. The work at the bottom of the ship caused him to catch a terrible chill which turned into a fever, and after some days of suffering he lay in his hammock close to the door of death. He wasted and wasted away in those long-lingering days until there seemed but little left of him but his frame and tattooing. But as everything else in him grew thin and his cheekbones grew sharper, his eyes grew fuller and fuller.

Every man on the crew gave Queequeg but little

time to live, and as for Queequeg himself, what he thought of his chances was shown by a favor that he asked. He called one of the crew to him one morning just as day was breaking, and said that while in Nantucket he had seen certain little canoes of dark wood, like the rich war-wood of his native island. Upon asking, he had found out that all whalemen who died in Nantucket were laid in those same dark canoes, and he wished to be laid out in the same way. This was like the custom of his race, who, after embalming a dead warrior, stretched him out in his canoe, and so left him to float away. After saying this, he added that he hated to think of being buried in his hammock, as was the custom on the sea, and being tossed like something bad to the sharks. No, he wished a canoe like those used in Nantucket.

When it became known to the crew what the wishes of Queequeg were, the carpenter was at once ordered to follow Queequeg's orders, whatever they were. There was some coffin-colored old lumber aboard, and from these dark planks the coffin was to be made. No sooner had the carpenter been given the order, than, taking his rule, he went to Queequeg's hammock and took the harpooneer's measurements with great care.

"Ah! Poor fellow! He'll have to die now," said one of the sailors.

When the last nail was driven in the coffin and the lid was fitted, the carpenter shouldered the coffin and went forward with it, inquiring whether the box was needed at this time. Members of the crew who were on deck at the time told the carpenter to take the coffin away since Queequeg was still alive. But Queequeg, hearing the talk, ordered the coffin to be brought to him at once. And so his orders were obeyed.

Leaning over in his hammock, Queequeg watched the coffin for a long time. He then called for his harpoon, had the wooden handle taken from it, and then had the iron part placed in the coffin along with the paddles of his boat. All by his own request, also, biscuits were then ranged round the sides within, and a flask of fresh water was placed at the head. A piece of sail cloth being rolled up for a pillow, Queequeg now asked to be lifted into his final bed to test its comforts, if any it had.

He lay a few minutes without moving, and then he ordered that his little god Yojo be brought to him. Then crossing his arms on his breast, with Yojo between, he called for the coffin lid to be placed over him. The head part turned over with a leather hinge, and there lay Queequeg in his coffin with little more than his face in view. "It will do," he said at last, and asked to be replaced in his hammock, a wish which was carried out.

But now that Queequeg had made every preparation for death and now that his coffin proved such a good fit, Queequeg suddenly became better. There was no need for the carpenter's box. Queequeg said he had changed his mind about dying. It was Queequeg's belief that if a man made up his mind to live, sickness could not kill him. Nothing but a whale or a storm, or something like that could take the life of a man.

There is a great deal of difference between a savage and a civilized person. It may take a civilized man six months to mend after a sickness, but a sick savage is well again in a day or two. So, in good time, my Queequeg gained strength, and after a few days of rest, gave himself a good stretching, sprang into the head of a boat, and taking a harpoon, said he was ready to fight a whale.

He now used his coffin for a sea chest, and emptying into it his canvas bag of clothes, set them in order there. Many hours he spent in carving the lid with all manner of figures and drawings, and it seemed he was trying in his rude way to copy parts of the twisted tattooings on his body.

29 *Perth Welds a Harpoon for Ahab*

When gliding past the Bashee Islands, we came at last upon the great South Sea,[1] a part of the world I often had longed to see. The quiet ocean rolled eastward from me for a thousand leagues of blue. It is the middle of all the waters of the world, the Indian Ocean and the Atlantic Ocean being its arms.

But Ahab was not interested in the beauty and extent of the South Sea. He was thinking of the hated white whale, which must even then be swimming in these waters. Having arrived at the waters where he would most likely find Moby Dick, the old man was even more determined than ever. His firm lips met like the lips of a vise, and his forehead's veins swelled like an overflowing brook. In his sleep his ringing cry ran through the ship, "Stern all! The white whale spouts thick blood!"

Because the weather was summer-cool, Perth, the blistered old blacksmith, kept his forge [2] on deck, where it was easy to do the many jobs of altering, repairing, or shaping weapons and boat furniture. Often he would be surrounded by an eager circle, all waiting to be served while they held boat-spades, pike-heads, harpoons,

[1] The southern part of the Pacific Ocean.
[2] A small furnace.

176

and lances, and watching every sooty movement as he toiled.

A peculiar walk in this old man had early in the voyage caused the crew to be curious, and he finally had told them the shameful story of his wretched fate. One bitter winter's midnight, on a road running between two country towns, the blacksmith felt a deadly numbness stealing over him, and sought shelter in an old barn. Because of the cold, he lost the toes from both feet, and this was the cause of his peculiar walk.

Perth had been a good blacksmith, with plenty to do. He owned a house and garden, had a youthful, daughter-like, loving wife, and three ruddy children, and every Sunday went to a cheerful-looking church in a grove. But one night under the cover of darkness, a desperate burglar slid into his happy home and robbed them all of everything. The burglar was drink, and the blacksmith was not strong enough to drive him away. Upon the opening of that fatal cork, the burglar came out and broke up his home.

The blacksmith's shop was in the basement of his dwelling, but with a separate entrance to it, so that always had the young and living healthy wife listened with pleasure to the stout ringing of her young-armed old husband's hammer. But the blows of the basement hammer every day grew more and more seldom, and each blow every day grew fainter than the last. The wife sat frozen at the window, with tearless eyes, gazing into the weeping faces of her children. The bellows fell, the forge choked up with cinders, the house was sold, and the mother soon died, as did two of the children. The old man staggered off, a tramp, and death seemed to be the only end for him.

But the ocean said to Perth, "Come hither, broken-

hearted. Here is another life." Hearing this voice by early sunrise and by fall of evening, the blacksmith responded, "Here I come." And so Perth went a-whaling.

With matted beard and clothed in a sharkskin apron, about the middle of the day Perth was standing between his forge and anvil when Captain Ahab came along, carrying in his hand a small, rusty-looking leather bag. "What wert thou making there?" Ahab asked Perth.

"Welding an old pike head, sir. There were seams, and dents in it."

"And canst thou make it all smooth again, blacksmith, after it has been used so roughly?"

"I think so, sir."

"And I suppose thou canst smooth almost any seams and dents, never mind how hard the metal, blacksmith?"

"Aye, sir, I think I can."

"Look ye here!" said Ahab, jingling the leather bag as if it were full of coins. "I, too, want a harpoon made, one that can not be torn apart, Perth, something that will stick in a whale like his own fin bone. There's the stuff!" And he flung the leather pouch upon the anvil. "Look ye, blacksmith, these are the gathered nail stubs of the steel shoes of racing horses."

"Horseshoe stubs, sir? Why Captain Ahab, thou hast here, then, the best and toughest stuff we blacksmiths ever work."

"I know it, old man. These stubs will weld together like glue from the melted bones of murderers. Quick! Forge me the harpoon. And forge me first twelve rods for the lower part. Then wind and twist and hammer these twelve together like yarns and strands of a tow line. Quick! I'll blow the fire."

When at last the twelve rods were made, Ahab tried them, one by one, with his own hand. "Here is a bad one," he told Perth. "Work that over again." This done, Perth was about to begin welding the twelve into one when Ahab stopped him, and said he would weld his own iron. At last the lower part, in one complete rod, received its final heat, and as Perth, to temper it, plunged it all hissing into the cask of water nearby, the scalding steam shot up into Ahab's bent face.

"Wouldst thou burn me, Perth?" cried Ahab.

"Pray God, not that. Yet I fear something, Captain Ahab. Is not this harpoon for the white whale?"

"Yes, for the white devil! But now for the barbs. Thou must make them thyself, man. Here are my razors—the best of steel. Make the barbs as sharp as the needle sleet of the icy sea." For a moment the old blacksmith eyed the razors as if he did not wish to use them.

"Take them, man. I have no need for them. Get to work," Ahab ordered.

Fashioned at last into the shape of an arrow and welded by Perth to the lower part, the harpoon was almost finished. As the blacksmith was giving the barbs their final heat, before tempering them, Perth asked Ahab to place the water cask near.

"No, no, no water for that. I want it of the true death-temper. Ahoy, there! Tashtego, Queequeg, Daggoo! What say ye, pagans! Will ye give me enough blood to cover this barb?" He held the newly made harpoon high up.

When the harpooneers replied, "Yes," three punctures were made in the heathen flesh and the white whale's barbs were then tempered.

Now, taking the spare poles from below and selecting one of hickory, with the bark still clinging to it, Ahab fitted the end to the socket of the iron. Ahab then tied to the weapon a coil of new tow-line. The harpoon finished, Ahab walked away carrying the weapon, the sound of his ivory leg and the sound of the hickory pole ringing along the deck.

30 *The* Pequod *Meets the* Bachelor

Jolly enough were the sights and sounds that came bearing down before the wind some weeks after Ahab's harpoon had been welded. It was a Nantucket ship, the *Bachelor*, which had just taken in her last cask of oil, and now, ready to go home, was sailing around among the widely-separated vessels. The three men at her masthead wore long streamers of narrow red bunting on their hats, and from the stern a whale boat was suspended, bottom down. Hanging captive was seen the long lower jaw of the last whale they had slain. Signals and flags of all colors were flying from her sides.

As was afterwards learned, the *Bachelor* had met with the most surprising success. And it was all the more wonderful, for that while cruising in the same seas, many other vessels had gone entire months without catching a single fish. Not only had barrels of beef and bread been given away to make room for the far more valuable sperm, but additional barrels had been traded from the ships the *Bachelor* had met, and these had been stored along the deck and in the captain's and officers' rooms.

As the *Bachelor* bore down upon the *Pequod*, Ahab's men saw that there was much merrymaking aboard the former. Those on the *Bachelor* who weren't dancing and merrymaking were busy pulling down the masonry of the try-works [1] and casting it into the sea, since it was no longer of any use because the ship had aboard all the oil it could carry.

Lord and master over all this scene, the captain of the *Bachelor* stood watching on the ship's quarter-deck. And Ahab, too, was standing on his quarter-deck as the two ships came close together.

"Come aboard, come aboard!" cried the gay *Bachelor*'s commander, lifting a glass and a bottle in the air.

"Hast seen the white whale?" gritted Ahab in reply.

"No, only heard of him, but don't believe in him at all," said the other smiling. "Come aboard!"

"Thou art too jolly. Sail on. Hast lost any men?"

"Not enough to speak of, two, that's all. But come aboard, old hearty, come along. I'll soon make you happy."

"What a fool!" muttered Ahab. Then he said aloud, "Thou art a full ship and homeward bound, thou sayest. Well, then, call me an empty ship and outward bound. So go thy way, and I will mine. Forward there! Set all sail, and keep her to the wind!"

And thus while one ship went cheerily before the breeze, the other stubbornly fought against it, and so the two vessels parted. The crew of the *Pequod* looked sadly at the homeward-bound *Bachelor*, and the crew of the *Bachelor* continued with their merrymaking.

The next day after the *Pequod* met the *Bachelor*, whales were seen and four were slain, one of them by Ahab. The four whales slain that late afternoon had died wide apart, and only three of them could be brought to the ship before nightfall. The other had to be left until

---

[1] Stone furnace used for cooking the oil from the whale blubber where the try-pots are hung.

the next morning, and the boat that killed it, Ahab's, lay by its side all night. A pole was placed upright into the dead whale's spouthole, and a lantern was hung on the pole. Only Fedallah kept a close lookout for sharks. The gray dawn came on, the slumbering crew arose from the boat's bottom, and before noon the dead whale was brought to the ship.

The season for the Line, an area known to be good hunting ground for whales, drew near, and many of the men would stand with their eyes fixed on the nailed doubloon. They were eager for the order to point the ship toward the equator, and in good time the order came. Now in the Japanese Sea at this time of year, the sky looks as if it were painted. Clouds there are none. Ahab looked upward toward the sun and murmured to himself, "Thou high and mighty Pilot! Thou tellest me truly where I am, but canst thou cast the least hint where I shall be? Where is Moby Dick? This instant thou must be seeing him."

Then Ahab picked up the quadrant [2] and said to it, "Curse thee, thou toy; curse thee, thou quadrant," and so saying the mad Ahab dashed it to the deck. "No longer will I guide my earthly way by thee. The compass shall conduct me and show me my place on the sea and the way to Moby Dick!"

[2] An instrument for determining position.

31 *A Storm Hits Us*

Skies that are mild and beautiful sometimes carry the most deadly storms. Pretty Cuba knows tornadoes that never swept the tame northern lands. So it is in these beautiful Japanese seas that the sailor sometimes meets the worst of all storms, the typhoon. It will sometimes burst from out the cloudless sky like an exploding bomb upon a dazed and sleepy town.

Toward evening of that day, the *Pequod* was torn of her canvas, and was left to fight a typhoon that struck her directly ahead. When darkness came on, sky and sea roared and split with the thunder and blazed with the lightning that showed the disabled masts fluttering here and there with sails torn into rags. Starbuck was standing on the quarter-deck trying to measure the damage by the light produced by lightning flashes. Stubb and Flask were directing the men in tying the boats more securely, but their work was doing very little good. A great rolling sea, dashing high up against the ship, stove in the bottom of Ahab's boat, and left it like a sieve.

"Bad work, bad work, Mr. Starbuck," said Stubb regarding the wreck, "but the sea will have its way. Stubb, for one, can't fight it. You see, Mr. Starbuck, a wave has such a great long start before it leaps; all round the world it runs, and then comes the spring! But as for me, all the start I have to meet it is just across the deck here. But never mind, it's all in fun, so the old song says." (Stubb sings.)

> Oh! jolly is the gale,
> And a joker is the whale,
> A' flourishing his tail—

Such a funny, sporty, gamy, jesty, joky, hoky-poky lad is the Ocean, oh!

> The scud all a-flyin',
> That's his flip only foamin';
> When he stirs in the spicin'—

Such a funny, sporty, gamy, jesty, joky, hoky-poky lad is the Ocean, oh!

> Thunder splits the ships,
> But he only smacks his lips,
> A tastin' of this flip—

Such a funny, sporty, gamy, jesty, joky, hoky-poky lad is the Ocean, oh!

"Stop, Stubb!" cried Starbuck. "Let the typhoon sing and strike his harp here in our rigging, but if thou art a brave man, thou will keep quiet."

"But I am not a brave man; never said I was a brave man. I am a coward, and I sing to keep up my spirits. And I tell you, Mr. Starbuck, there's no way to stop my singing in this world but to cut my throat!"

"Here!" cried Starbuck, changing the subject and seizing Stubb by the shoulder. "Do you notice that the storm comes from the east, the very route Ahab is to run to find Moby Dick?"

"I don't half understand ye. What's in the wind?"

"Around the Cape of Good Hope is the shortest way to Nantucket," explained Starbuck. "We can turn the storm that now hammers at us into a fair wind, one that will take us home, if we but turn around. Against the wind all is blackness. Away from it there is light but not lightning." At that moment, which was entirely dark, a voice was heard, and almost at the same time thunder rolled overhead.

"Who's there?" Starbuck questioned.

"Old Thunder!" said Ahab, feeling his way along the bulwarks to his pivot hole and finding his path made plain to him by the lightning.

Now as the lightning rod to a building on shore is intended to carry off the fire into the soil, so the lightning rod on a ship is intended to carry off the lightning into the water. Because the lower part of a ship's lightning rods must be placed into the water at a great depth, they hinder the progress of the ship in the water. Thus, the lower parts of the rods are usually kept on board to be thrown out when a storm appears.

"The rods! The rods!" cried Starbuck to the crew, when the flashes came oftener and oftener. "Are they overboard? Drop them over. Quick!"

"Stop!" cried Ahab. "Let the rods stay where they are, sir."

"Look above!" shouted Starbuck. "The corposants.[1] The corposants!" The highest points of the ship were tipped with a dull fire; and touched at each lightning rod with three tapering white flames, each of the three tall masts was silently burning like three huge candles before an altar.

"The corposants have mercy on us all!" cried Stubb in a serious tone. While the fire was burning above, few words were heard from the frightened crew, who in one thick cluster stood on the forecastle, all of their eyes gleaming.

A moment or two passed, when Starbuck, going forward, pushed against someone. It was Stubb. "What thinkest thou now, man? I heard thy cry. It was not the same as in the song."

"No, no, it wasn't. I said the corposants have mercy on us all, and I hope they will, still. And look ye, Mr. Starbuck—but it's too dark to look. Hear me then, I take

---

[1] Flamelike electricity which sometimes appears at the high points of a ship during a storm.

that masthead flame we saw for a sign of good luck. See! See! The corposants have mercy on us all!"

"Aye, aye, men!" shouted Ahab. "Look up at it. Mark it well. The white flame lights the way to the white whale."

"The boat! The boat!" cried Starbuck. "Look at thy boat, old man!" From Ahab's harpoon, the one forged at Perth's fire, came a flame of pale, forked fire.

As the silent harpoon burned there like a serpent's tongue, Starbuck grasped Ahab by the arm, saying, "God, God is against thee, old man. Stop! 'Tis an ill voyage, ill begun, ill continued. While we may, old man, let us turn homeward."

Overhearing Starbuck, the panic-stricken crew raised a cry that seemed to mean they would not obey Ahab's orders any longer. But snatching the burning harpoon, Ahab waved it like a torch among them, swearing he would kill the first sailor who attempted to change the sails. Afraid of Ahab's face and shrinking from the fiery harpoon, the men fell back, and Ahab again spoke: "All your oaths to hunt the white whale are as binding as mine, and by heart, soul, body, lungs, and life, old Ahab is bound. And that ye may know to what tune this heart beats, look ye here. Thus I blow out the last fear." And with one blast of breath he extinguished the flame.

At those last words of Ahab's, many of the sailors, even more frightened, ran from him.

32 Starbuck Is Tempted

During the most violent shocks of the typhoon, the man at the *Pequod*'s tiller had several times been hurled to the deck. In a severe storm like this, while the ship is tossed about by the blast, it is by no means uncommon to see the needles in the compasses go round and round.

Some hours after midnight, the storm had calmed down so much that Starbuck and Stubb were able to cut adrift the pieces of sail that had been torn to shreds by the terrific wind. New sails were then run up, and soon the ship went easily through the water again. The helmsman was given the order to steer east-southeast again, for during the storm, he had steered whatever way seemed the best. As the ship was brought as near her course as possible, the foul breeze became fair, and this cheered the sailors.

At once the sails were squared to the lively song of "Ho! the fair wind! Oh-he-yo, cheerily men!" Everyone seemed happy again.

It was Ahab's order that any changes on the ship should be reported to him immediately, and Starbuck had no sooner set the sails, even though he had no stomach for the voyage now, than he went below to tell Ahab of what had been done.

But before knocking at Ahab's stateroom, he paused a moment. The cabin lamp—taking long swings this way and that—was casting shadows upon the old man's door. The loaded muskets in the rack were shown as they stood up against the forward bulkhead. Starbuck was an honest, upright man, but out of his heart, at that instant when he saw the muskets, there came an evil thought.

"He would have shot me once," he murmured. "Yes, there's the very musket that he pointed at me. Let me touch it—lift it. Strange that I, who have handled so many deadly lances, strange that I should shake so now. Is it loaded? I must see. I must not think of shooting Ahab. I have come to report to him that there is a fair wind. But how fair? Is it not to mean death for all of us? Perhaps it's only fair for Moby Dick. The very gun he pointed at me! The very one, this one—I hold it here. He would have killed me with the very thing I handle now. Yes, even all the crew!

"Did he not break the quadrant? In this very typhoon did he not swear that he would have no lightning rods? But shall this crazed old man be allowed to drag a whole ship's company to death with him? Yes, it would make him the murderer of thirty men and more if the ship comes to any deadly harm. And come to deadly harm, my soul swears, this ship will if Ahab has his way. If then, I should kill him, that crime would not be his.

"Yes, just there, in there, he's sleeping. Sleeping? Aye, but still alive and soon awake again. But is there no other way than killing him? No lawful way? Make him a prisoner to be taken home? What hope to wrest this old man's living power from his own living hands? Only a fool would try it. Say he were tied down, knotted over with ropes and chained down to ringbolts on this cabin floor; he would be more hideous than a caged tiger. I could not endure the sight, and would not be able to sleep.

"What then remains? The land is hundreds of leagues away, and locked Japan is the nearest. I stand alone here upon an open sea, with two oceans and a whole continent between me and the law. Is heaven a murderer when its lightning strikes a would-be murderer in his bed, and would I be a murderer then if—" and slowly, stealthily, and half sideways looking, he placed the loaded musket's end against the door.

"On this level, Ahab's hammock swings within; his head this way. A pull on the trigger and Starbuck may live to hug his wife and child again. Oh, Mary! Mary! —boy! boy! boy! But if I do not kill thee, old man, who can tell when Starbuck's body may sink to the bottom of the ocean, with all the crew! Great God, where art thou? Shall I kill him? Shall I kill him?"

At this point Ahab spoke out in his sleep, "Oh, Moby Dick, I shall kill you at last!" Such were the sounds that came from the old man's tormented sleep.

The yet-leveled musket shook like a drunkard's arm against the panel, but Starbuck could not bring himself to kill the old man. He turned from the door, placed the musket in its rack, and left the place.

"He's too sound asleep, Mr. Stubb. You go down and wake him and tell him. I must see to the deck here. Thou knowest what to say."

Next morning the sea was still quite rough, and the wind pushed the *Pequod* ahead at great speed. Ahab, still silent, stood apart, but suddenly, struck by some thought, he hurried toward the helm and demanded how the ship was heading.

"East-sou'-east, sir," said the frightened steersman.

"Thou liest!" said Ahab, striking him with his clenched fists. "Heading east at this hour in the morning, and the sun to our backs?" What Ahab said was true, although no one else aboard had noticed it.

Ahab caught one glimpse of the compass; his uplifted arm slowly fell, and for a moment he almost seemed to stagger. Standing behind him, Starbuck looked, and lo! the two compasses pointed east and the *Pequod* was going west.

But before the first wild alarm could get out aboard among the crew, the old man with a laugh exclaimed, "I have it! It has happened before. Mr. Starbuck, last night's thunder turned our compasses—that's all. Thou hast before now heard of such a thing, I take it."

"Yes, but never before has it happened to me, sir," said the pale Starbuck.

It must be said that accidents like this have in more than one case happened to ships in violent storms. In instances where the lightning has actually struck the vessel, so as to strike down the spars and rigging, the compass becomes of no more use than an old wife's knitting needle. But in either case, the needle never again is of any use in guiding the ship.

Watching the damaged compasses, Ahab, with his extended hand, now took the bearing of the sun, and satisfied that the needles were pointing in the exactly opposite direction, shouted out his orders for the ship's course to be changed.

Whatever were his own secret thoughts, Starbuck said nothing, but carried out Ahab's orders, and Stubb and Flask did likewise. As for the men, though some of them grumbled, their fear of Ahab was greater than their fear of fate. But there was no sign of unrest from the pagan harpooneers.

Ahab knew well that he needed to revive the spirit of his crew, since sailors are very superstitious when something happens to the compass needles. "Men," said he, steadily turning upon the crew after Starbuck had handed him some materials. "Men, the thunder turned old Ahab's needles, but out of a bit of steel Ahab can make a compass of his own, one that will point as true as any." The sailors looked in wonder and waited for whatever magic might follow, but Starbuck looked away. Then with a hammer, a piece of steel, and linen thread, Ahab put together a homemade compass.

At first the steel went round and round, but at last it settled to its place. Ahab, who had been intently watching for this result, stepped back and pointing his stretched arm toward it, exclaimed, "Look ye for yourselves! The sun is east and my compass shows that." One after another the crew looked at the compass, and one after another they dropped away.

Steering now southeastward by Ahab's compass, the *Pequod* held on her path toward the equator. At last the ship drew near the outskirts of the equatorial fishing ground, and in the deep darkness that goes before the dawn, was sailing by a cluster of rocky islands. The watch, then headed by Flask, was startled by a cry so wild and unearthly that one and all, aroused by the sound, stood up to listen. Some of the crew said it was mermaids and shuddered, but the pagan harpooneers were not disturbed. The oldest sailor of them all declared that the wild thrilling sounds that were heard were the voices of newly drowned men in the sea.

Below in his hammock, Ahab did not hear of this until dawn, when he came to the deck. When Flask told him of the terrible noises that were heard, Ahab hollowly laughed, and explained that those rocky islands the ship had passed were the home of great numbers of seals. Some young seals, he said, had lost their mothers and were crying and sobbing with their human sort of wail. But this only frightened some of the sailors more, because most of them were very superstitious about seals. This superstition had come about not only from the particular sounds the seals made when in distress but also from the human look of their round heads and faces as seen from the water alongside the ship. In the sea, under certain circumstances, seals have more than once been mistaken for men.

The crew became even more fearful at something which happened the next morning. At sunrise one man, who may have been half asleep, went from his hammock to the masthead, and he had not been long at the lookout when a cry was heard. Looking up, the crew saw a falling phantom in the air, and looking down, saw a little tossed heap of white bubbles in the blue of the sea. The lifebuoy was dropped to the place where the sailor had sunk, but no hand rose to seize it. Then the lifebuoy, which had been exposed to the sun so long, filled up with water and sank, following the man to the bottom of the ocean, as if to make him a pillow.

And thus the first man of the *Pequod* that mounted the mast to look out for the white whale, on the white whale's own ground, was swallowed up in the deep. But few, perhaps, thought of that at the time. They declared that now they knew the reason for those wild shrieks they had heard the night before.

Starbuck was directed to see that the lost lifebuoy was replaced, but no barrel of sufficient lightness could be found. Thus it seemed that there would be no lifebuoy until Queequeg hinted a hint concerning his coffin.

"A lifebuoy of a coffin!" cried Starbuck, starting.

"Rather queer, I should say," said Stubb.

"It will make a good enough one," said Flask. "The carpenter here can arrange it easily."

"Bring it up. There's nothing else for it," said Starbuck after a pause. "Rig it, carpenter, but do not look at me so—the coffin I mean. Dost thou hear me? Rig it."

"And shall I nail down the lid, sir?" asked the carpenter, moving his hand as with a hammer.

"Yes."

"And shall I seal the seams, sir?" He moved his hand as with a sealing iron.

"Yes. Away! Make a lifebuoy of the coffin and no more. Mr. Stubb, Mr. Flask, come forward with me."

"Starbuck is angry," said the carpenter. "Now I don't like this. I make a leg for Captain Ahab, and he wears it like a gentleman, but I make a bandbox for Queequeg, and he won't put his head into it. Are all my pains to go for nothing with that coffin? And now I'm ordered to make a lifebuoy of it. It's like turning an old coat; I don't like this sort of business. I don't like it at all; it's not my place. Let me see. Nail down the lid, seal the seams, and hang it over the side of the ship. Were ever such things done before with a coffin? But I'll do the job. I'll have me—let's see—how many in the ship's company altogether? But I've forgotten. Anyway, I'll have me thirty separate lifelines, each three feet long hanging all around the coffin. Then if the ship goes down, there'll be thirty lively fellows all fighting for one coffin, a sight not seen very often beneath the sun. Come hammer, sealing iron, pitch pot—let's to it!"

33 We Find the Wake[1] of Moby Dick

Next day a large ship, the *Rachel,* all her spars thickly clustering with men, was seen bearing directly down upon the *Pequod.* At the time the *Pequod* was making good speed through the water, but as the stranger shot close to her, the sails of both ships fell together.

"Bad news, she brings bad news," muttered one of the sailors. But before her commander, with trumpet to mouth, could say anything, Ahab's voice was heard.

"Hast seen the white whale?"

"Yes, yesterday. Have ye seen a whale boat adrift?" The news of Moby Dick made Ahab happy, it was plain to see, as he told the commander of the *Rachel* that the *Pequod* had seen no whale boat adrift. Ahab would have boarded the stranger vessel, but the captain of the *Rachel* was seen preparing to come aboard the *Pequod.* A few keen pulls, and he sprang to the deck. Immediately he was recognized by Ahab for a Nantucketer he knew.

"Where was Moby Dick? Not killed! Not killed!" cried Ahab, closely advancing. "How was it?"

It seemed that somewhat late on the afternoon of the day before, three of the stranger's boats had been in pursuit of a number of whales which had led them some

[1] Track or course.

four or five miles from the ship. And while they were in swift chase, the white hump and head of Moby Dick had suddenly loomed up out of the blue water, and a fourth boat was sent after him. After a keen sail before the wind, the fourth boat seemed to have succeeded in fastening to the white whale; at least that is the way it seemed to the man at the masthead. In the distance he saw the boat, and then a swift gleam of bubbling white water. After that nothing more could be seen, and it was decided that the whale must have run away with the boat, as often happens.

The recall signals were placed in the rigging, and the three other boats were picked up as darkness came on. With the rest of the crew being safe aboard, the *Rachel* crowded all sail after the missing boat, kindling a fire in her try-pots for a beacon, and every man was on the lookout. Though she had sailed to the spot where the boat was supposed to be, and the boats were lowered for additional search, not a trace of the missing boat could be found.

The story told, the stranger captain at once told his reason for boarding the *Pequod*. He wished the ship to unite with the *Rachel* in the search by sailing over the sea some four or five miles apart. "I will bet something now," whispered Stubb to Flask, "that someone in that missing boat wore off the captain's best coat. Perhaps his watch, and he's anxious to get it back. Whoever heard of two whale ships cruising after one missing whale boat in the height of the whaling season! See, Flask, how pale he looks. It must have been the—"

"My boy, my own son is among them," exclaimed the stranger captain. "For God's sake—I beg. For eight and forty hours let me hire your ship. I will gladly pay for it. You *shall* do this thing."

"His son!" cried Stubb. "Oh, it's his son he's lost! I take back the coat and watch. What says Ahab? We must save that boy."

"He drowned with the rest of them last night," said the old sailor. "I heard; all of ye heard their spirits." The missing lad, who was but twelve years old, had been taken aboard at that early age by his father to accustom him to the sea. It sometimes happens that Nantucket captains will send a son so young for a three or four years' voyage on some ship other than their own.

The stranger captain still continued to beg Ahab, but the old man stood like an anvil. "I will not go," said the stranger, "until you say aye to me. Do to me as you would have me do to you in the like case. For you, too, have a boy, Captain Ahab, though but a child, and nestling safely at home now. Yes, yes, I see you are going to do it. Run, run, men, and stand by to change the course of the ship."

"Stop," cried Ahab. "Touch not a rope yarn." Then he said, "Captain Gardiner, I will not do it. Even now I lose time. Good-bye, good-bye. God bless ye, man, and may I forgive myself, but I must go. Mr. Starbuck, in three minutes see that all strangers are off the ship, and then let the ship sail as before."

Then turning his face downward, Ahab went into his cabin, leaving the strange captain shocked at the decision. Captain Gardiner, silent, hurried to the side, more fell than stepped into his boat, and returned to his ship. Soon the stranger ship slipped away, but in so doing, she was seen to search every dark spot on the sea for the missing boat. But the *Rachel* could not find her children.

Ahab, all other whaling waters having been swept, seemed to have chased Moby Dick into the very place where the white whale had taken off his leg. Moby Dick was known to be near, for had not the *Rachel* just seen him! The crew was gloomy; Stubb no more smiled. Like machines, the crew moved about the deck, always aware that the old man's eye was upon them. At any time, by night or day, the sailors stepped on deck Ahab was before them. For days and nights he had not slept in his hammock, yet they could never tell whether his eyes were closed at times or whether he was still looking. Day by day and night after night, he went no more to his cabin; whatever he wanted from the cabin he sent for.

He ate in the same open air; that is, his only two meals, breakfast and dinner. Supper he never touched. At the first faintest glimmering of the dawn, his iron voice was heard, "Man the mastheads!" And all through the day until after sunset and after twilight, the same voice sounded every hour, "What d'ye see? Look sharp! Sharp!"

But when three or four days had passed, after meeting the children-seeking *Rachel,* and no spout had been seen, the old man began to lose faith in his crew, with the exception of his pagan harpooneers. He seemed to think that Stubb and Flask might purposely overlook Moby Dick. However, Ahab said nothing about his loss of faith in part of the crew.

"I will have the first sight of the whale myself," Ahab said. "Yes, Ahab must have the doubloon!" Then placing himself in a basket, he gave the word for them to hoist him to his perch, Starbuck tying the rope and watching it. And thus, with one hand clinging around the royal mast, Ahab gazed at the sea for miles and miles, this side and that, within the wide circle commanded at so great a height.

When a man is sent aloft and is held there by rope, its fastened end on deck is given to someone in strict charge of it. So it was with Ahab; the only strange thing about it seemed to be that Starbuck, almost the only man who had ever dared oppose him in anything and whose faithfulness he doubted, was the very man he should select for his watchman. Thus Ahab was giving his whole life into the hands of a person he distrusted.

Now the first time Ahab was perched aloft, before

he had been there ten minutes, one of those red-billed savage sea hawks came wheeling and screaming around his head in a number of swift circlings. Then it darted a thousand feet straight up into the air and came down and circled round Ahab's head. But with his gaze fixed upon the dim and distant horizon, Ahab seemed not to notice this wild bird. Nor, in most cases would anyone else have noticed it, except at this time, everyone seemed to see some sort of meaning in almost every sight.

"Your hat, your hat, sir!" suddenly cried a seaman who was posted at a masthead directly behind Ahab. But already the bird was before the old man's eyes, the long hooked bill was at his head, and the black hawk darted away with Ahab's hat.

The *Pequod* sailed on, the rolling waves and days went by, the lifebuoy coffin still lightly swung, and another ship, the *Delight*, was met. As she drew near, all eyes were fixed upon her broad beams, which, in some whaling ships, cross the quarter-deck at the height of eight or nine feet and carry the spare or unrigged boats. Upon these beams were seen the shattered, white ribs and some splintered planks of what had once been a whale boat, but you now see through this wreck, as plainly as you see through the skeleton of a horse.

"Hast seen the white whale?"

"Look!" replied the hollow-cheeked captain, and with his trumpet pointed to the wreck.

"Hast killed him?"

"The harpoon is not yet forged that will ever do that," answered the other, sadly glancing upon a rounded hammock on the deck, whose gathered sides some noiseless sailors were busy sewing together.

"Not forged!" And snatching Perth's leveled iron, Ahab held it out, exclaiming, "Look ye, Nantucketer. Here in this hand I hold his death! Tempered in blood and tempered by lightning are these barbs, and I swear to temper them again in that hot place behind the fin, where the White Whale feels his life most."

"Then God keep thee, old man—see'st thou that?" He pointed to the hammock. "I bury but one of five stout men who were alive only yesterday, but were dead before night. Only *that* one I bury; the rest were buried before they died. You sail upon their tomb." Then turning to his crew—"Are you ready? Place the plank then on the rail and lift the body; so then—Oh! God!" advancing toward the hammock with uplifted hands—"may the resurrection and the life—"

"Brace forward, start the ship!" cried Ahab like lightning to his men. But the suddenly started *Pequod* was not quick enough to escape the sound of the splash that the corpse made as it struck the sea. As Ahab now glided from the sad *Delight*, the strange lifebuoy hanging at the *Pequod*'s side again came into view.

34 *Starbuck Longs for Home*

It was a clear steel-blue day. Here and there on high glided the snow-white wings of small, unspeckled birds, but far down in the bottomless sea rushed the swordfish and sharks, the murderers of the ocean.

Tied up and twisted and knotted with wrinkles, his eyes glowing like coals, Ahab stood forth in the clearness of the morn. From beneath his slouched hat Ahab dropped a tear into the sea; and all the Pacific did not contain such wealth as that one wee drop. Starbuck saw the old man; saw how heavily he leaned over the side. Careful not to touch him, or be noticed by him, Starbuck drew near and stood there.

Ahab turned.

"Starbuck!"

"Sir."

"Oh, Starbuck, it is a mild, mild wind and a mild-looking sky. On such a day as this, when I was only eighteen, I struck my first whale. Forty, forty, forty years ago! Forty years of whaling! Forty years of danger and storm! Forty years on the pitiless sea! For forty years has Ahab left the peaceful land to make wars on the horrors of the deep! Yes, Starbuck, out of those forty years I have not spent three ashore. Then I think of this life I have led, think of the dry salted food and of being oceans away from that young girl-wife I, past fifty, wedded. Yes, I made a widow of the poor girl when I married her, Starbuck. Yes, yes, what a forty years' fool, fool, old fool has old Ahab been! But do I look very old, so very, very old, Starbuck?

"Close! Stand close to me, Starbuck. Let me look into your eyes. It is better than to gaze into sea or sky. I see my wife and child in your eyes, Starbuck. And when the time comes to give chase to Moby Dick, you shall stay on board, safe. No, not with that far-away home I see in your eye!"

"Oh, my captain! My captain! Noble soul! Grand old heart; after all, why should anyone give chase to that hated fish! Let us leave these deadly waters! Let us go home! Starbuck has a wife and child, too. Away, let us away! This instant let me change the course. How wonderful would it be to be on our way to see old Nantucket again. I think, sir, they have some such mild blue days, even as this, in Nantucket."

"They have, they have. I have seen them on summer days in the morning. About this time—yes, it is his noon nap now—the boy wakes, sits up in bed, and his mother tells him of me, how I am upon the deep but will yet come back to dance him again."

" 'Tis my Mary, my Mary herself!" shouted Starbuck. "She promised my boy that she would every morning carry him to the hill to catch the first glimpse of his father's sail! Yes, yes, no more, it is done! We head for Nantucket! Come, my captain, study out the course, and let us away! See, see! the boy's face from the window, the boy's hand on the hill!"

But Ahab turned his head, and it was plain to see that he would not give up the chase for Moby Dick. "What causes me," he said, "against lovings and longings, to keep pushing, crowding, jamming myself all the time? I am doing what I really know in my heart is not the proper thing to do!" Starbuck, turned ghostly pale, had stolen away.

35 *We Begin the Chase —First Day*

That night when old Ahab, as was his custom, stepped from his cabin and went to his pivot hole, he smelled the sea air and declared that a whale must be near. Soon that peculiar odor, which is sometimes given forth for a great distance by the living sperm whale, was noticed by all the crew. After inspecting the compass and figuring the exact place of the odor as nearly as possible, Ahab rapidly ordered the ship's course to be slightly changed.

At daybreak there was noticed a long sleek on the sea, as smooth as oil. "Man the mastheads! Call all hands!" blasted Ahab.

Thundering with the butts of three clubbed hand-spikes on the deck, Daggoo roused the sleepers with such loud claps that they almost instantly appeared on deck with their clothes in their hands.

"What d'ye see?" cried Ahab, flattening his face to the sky.

"Nothing, sir, nothing!" was the sound coming down in reply.

In a few moments Ahab was being hoisted to the mainmast; but while only two-thirds of the way up, he raised a cry in the air, "There she blows! There she blows! A hump like a snowhill! It is Moby Dick!"

Fired by the cry which was taken up by the three

lookouts, the men on deck rushed to the rigging to see the famous whale that they had so long been seeking. Ahab had now gained his final perch, some feet above the other lookouts, with Tashtego standing just beneath him, almost on a level with Ahab's heel. From this very height the whale was now seen some mile or so ahead, at every roll of the sea revealing his high sparkling hump and regularly jetting his silent spout into the air. To the superstitious crew it seemed the same silent spout they had so long ago seen in the moonlit Atlantic and Indian Oceans.

"And did none of ye see it before?" cried Ahab, hailing the perched men around him.

"I saw him almost the same instant, sir, that Captain Ahab did, and I cried out," said Tashtego.

"Not the same instant; not the same—no, the gold doubloon is mine, I, only; none of ye could have seen the white whale first. There she blows! There she blows! There she blows! There again! There again!" he cried in long drawn tones which kept time with the spoutings of the whale. "He's going down! Stand by three boats. Mr. Starbuck, remember, stay on board and keep the ship. Steady, men, steady! There go flukes! No, no; only black water! All ready the boats there? Stand by! Stand by! Lower me, Mr. Starbuck; lower, lower,—quick, quicker!" And he slid through the air to the deck.

"He's heading right away from us and can not have seen the ship yet," cried Stubb.

"Stand by the braces! Boats, boats!" shouted Ahab.

Soon all the boats but Starbuck's were dropped, all the boat sails were set, and the paddles were plying with rippling swiftness, with Ahab's boat leading the chase.

Their light boats sped through the sea, but only slowly did they near Moby Dick. As they neared him, the ocean grew smooth, so smooth it seemed like a meadow. At length the hunters came so near Moby Dick that his entire dazzling hump was easily seen in a ring of greenish foam. Ahab saw the wrinkles of the white whale's head, which was slightly extended out of the water.

And thus, through the quietness of the tropical sea, Moby Dick moved on, withholding from sight the terribleness of his jaw. But soon the fore part of him rose slowly from the water; for an instant his whole body formed a high arch, like Virginia's Natural Bridge, and then he went out of sight. Hovering and dipping on the wing, the white sea fowls lingered over the whirling pool that he had left. With paddles down and the sheets of their sails adrift, the three boats now floated, awaiting the return of Moby Dick.

"An hour," said Ahab, and he gazed beyond the whale's place toward the dim blue spaces. It was only an instant; for again his eyes seemed whirling around in his head as he swept the watery circle. The breeze now freshened; the sea began to swell.

"The birds! The birds!" cried Tashtego.

In long Indian file, as when herons take wing, the white birds were now all flying toward Ahab's boat; and when within a few yards began fluttering over the water there. Their vision was keener than man's, because Ahab could discover no sign in the sea. But suddenly, as he looked down into the depths, he saw a white living spot, no bigger than a white weasel, coming to the top with great speed and becoming larger as it rose. Then it turned, and then there were plainly shown two long, crooked rows of white glistening teeth floating up from the bottom of the sea.

It was Moby Dick's open mouth and vast jaw, his huge bulk not showing because it was the same color as

the blue of the sea. The mouth opened beneath Ahab's boat like an open-doored marble tomb, and giving one sidelong sweep with his steering oar, Ahab whirled the boat away from the horrible scene. Then, calling upon Fedallah to change places with him, he went forward to the bows, and seizing Perth's harpoon, commanded his crew to grasp their oars and stand by for action.

The bluish pearl-white of the inside of the jaw was within six inches of Ahab's head, and reached higher than that. The white whale then shook the boat as a cat will sometimes shake a mouse. Fedallah gazed, crossed his arms, and appeared unafraid. While the whale remained beneath the boat, he could not be harpooned, and Ahab was furious because he was almost helpless in the very jaws he hated. Then Ahab seized the long jaw bone of the whale with his naked hands, but it slipped from him, and the whale, like a huge pair of scissors, bit the boat completely in two.

At the moment just before the boat was destroyed, Ahab, noticing what the whale intended to do as it raised its head, made one final effort to push the boat away from the whale's mouth. But only slipping farther into the whale's mouth and tilting over sideways as it slipped, the boat had shaken off his hold on the jaw, had spilled him out of it as he leaned to push, and so Ahab fell flat-faced upon the sea. The destruction of the boat also dashed the crew into the sea, but they soon were hanging onto a piece of the wrecked vessel.

Withdrawing a short distance, Moby Dick thrust his white head up and down in the sea, so that when his vast wrinkled forehead rose some twenty or more feet out of the water, the waves broke against it and tossed spray high into the air. Then Moby Dick swam swiftly round and round the wrecked crew, churning the water, as if working himself up to another more deadly attack. The sight of the splintered boat seemed to madden him. Ahab, half smothered in the foam of the whale's tail, and too much of a cripple to swim, kept afloat even in the heart of such a whirlpool as that. Ahab's head looked like a tossed bubble which the least chance shock might burst.

Fedallah, hanging onto a piece of the boat, just watched Ahab, and the rest of the crew, clinging to the other end, could not rescue Ahab because it was more than enough for them to look to themselves. The whale, traveling in ever shorter circles, seemed to be swooping down upon them. And though the other boats, unharmed, still hovered close by, they dared not strike for fear that the whale would instantly destroy Ahab and his crew. At the same time, if that should happen, they themselves probably could not hope to escape. Thus, with straining eyes, they remained on the outer edge of the whale's circle, the center of which had now become Ahab's head.

The beginning of all this had been seen from the ship's mastheads, and she had come to the scene. So close was she to the whale that Ahab in the water hailed her, "Sail on the—" but at that moment a breaking sea caused by Moby Dick overwhelmed Ahab for a moment. But struggling out of it again, and rising on a wave, he shouted, "Sail on the whale! Drive him off!" The *Pequod* was pointed, and breaking up the circle, she parted the white whale from Ahab. As Moby Dick swam off, the boats flew to the rescue.

Dragged into Stubb's boat, Ahab, with bloodshot, blinded eyes, the white brine caking in his wrinkles, fell helpless into the bottom of the boat, like one trodden under foot of herds of elephants.

"The harpoon," said Ahab, halfway rising and drag-gingly leaning on one bended arm. "Is it safe?"

"Yes, sir, for it was not darted. This is it," said Stubb, showing it.

"Lay it before me. Any missing men?"

"One, two, three, four, five. There were five oars, sir and here are five men."

"That's good. Help me, man. I wish to stand. So, so, I see Moby Dick. There, There! What a leaping spout! Hands off me. Set the sail; out oars, and chase Moby Dick!"

It is often the case that when a boat is stove, its crew, being picked up by another boat, helps to work the second boat, and the chase is continued with double-banked oars. This was what happened in this case. But the added power of the boat did not equal the added power of the whale, for he seemed to have added strength in every fin. He swam with such speed that the chase seemed almost to be a hopeless one, because the crew could not endure for any long period such strain-ing at the oars. The ship itself seemed to be the most promising means of overtaking the whale, and the boats soon made for her and were taken up by the cranes. The two parts of the wrecked boat had been taken up before.

Then hoisting everything to her side and stacking her canvas high up, the *Pequod* bore down upon Moby Dick. From time to time the whale's glittering spout was announced from the manned mastheads. When the whale would be reported as just gone down, Ahab, watch in hand, would pace the deck until it was time for the whale to reappear again. When that time came, his voice was heard, "D'ye see him?" And if the reply was, "No, sir!" he would demand that they raise him to the masthead. In this way the day wore on, Ahab either on the masthead or pacing the planks.

As he was thus walking, uttering no sound except to hail the men aloft or to bid them hoist a sail still higher or to spread one to a greater breadth, he passed his own wrecked boat, which had been dropped upon the quarter-deck.

"Aye, sir," said Starbuck drawing near. "'Tis an omen, and an ill one."

But the wrecked boat did not stop Ahab in his pursuit of Moby Dick. "Omen?" he cried. "Begone! Above there! D'ye see him? Sing out for every spout, though he spout ten times a second!"

The day was nearly done and soon it was almost dark, but the lookout men still remained.

"Can't see the spout, now, sir. Too dark," cried a voice from the air.

"How heading when last seen?"

"Just the same as before, sir."

"Good! He will travel slower now that it is night. Take down some of the sails, Mr. Starbuck. We must not run over him before morning. Mr. Stubb, send a fresh hand to the foremost head and see that it is manned until morning." Then advancing toward the doubloon in the mainmast, he said, "Men, this gold is mine, for I earned it, but I shall let it stay here until the white whale is dead. And then whoever of ye first finds him on the day he shall be killed, this gold is that man's. If on that day I shall find him, then ten times its sum shall be divided among all of ye. Away now!"

And so saying, he placed himself halfway within the scuttle, and slouching his hat, stood there until dawn, except at the times he sought the time of night.

36 *The Chase Continues —Second Day*

At daybreak fresh men were placed at the three mastheads.

"D'ye see him?" cried Ahab a little while after daylight.

"See nothing, sir."

"Turn up all hands and make sail. He travels faster than I thought. The top sails! They should have been kept on her all night. But no matter. We are but resting for the rush."

Here be it said that the stubborn chase of one particular whale through day into night and through night into day is by no means unusual in the South Sea fishery. For Nantucket commanders know the habits of the whale so well that they can pretty accurately foretell both the direction he will continue to swim and his speed.

The ship tore on, leaving such a furrow in the sea as the ploughshare turns up in the level field.

"There she blows—she blows!—she blows!—right ahead!" was now the masthead cry.

"Yes, yes!" cried Stubb. "I knew it—ye can't escape. Blow on and split your spout, O whale. Ahab, the mad man himself is after ye! Blister your lungs, but Ahab will dam off your blood as a miller shuts his water gate upon the stream!"

The chase had by this time worked new enthusiasm into the crew. Whatever fears they may have had before were driven away not only by the sight of awful Ahab, but the excitement of the chase. They had been saved from the perils of the previous day, and the blind reckless way in which the ship pursued Moby Dick bowled their hearts along. The wind made great bellies of their sails and rushed the vessel along.

They were one man, not thirty. This man's valor and that man's fear were directed toward capturing Moby Dick. The rigging lived with men, and the mastheads were overspread with arms and legs. All the spars were full, ready for the fight with the white whale, the thing that might destroy them.

When the men reported that they could no longer see Moby Dick, Ahab told them they had been mistaken in reporting that they had seen him. "Swing me up, men. Mody Dick does not cast a jet and then disappear."

Ahab was right. In their eagerness, the men had mistaken some other thing for the whale spout. For hardly had Ahab reached his perch, hardly had the rope been tied to the deck, when thirty voices were heard. Much nearer to the ship than the place the imaginary jet had been seen, less than a mile ahead, Moby Dick burst bodily into view. Rising with much speed from the depths of the ocean, the sperm whale, like a mountain of dazzling foam, showed his entire bulk.

"There she breaches! There she breaches!" was the cry as the white whale tossed himself, salmon-like, on the water.

"Breach your last to the sun, Moby Dick!" cried Ahab. "Thy hour and thy harpoon are at hand! Down! Down, all of ye, but one man at the fore. The boats!

Stand by!" The men, like shooting stars, slid to the deck, while Ahab, not so rapidly, was dropped from his perch.

"Lower away!" he cried, as soon as he had reached his boat, a spare one which had been rigged the afternoon before. "Mr. Starbuck, the ship is thine. Keep away from the boats, but keep near them. Lower, all!"

As if to strike a quick terror into them, Moby Dick had turned and was now coming for the three crews. Ahab's boat was in the middle; and cheering his men, Ahab told them he would take the whale head-and-head. That is, he would pull straight up to his forehead, a common thing, because the whale sees much better from his sides than he does from in front, if an object is close at hand. But before the close limit was gained, the white whale churned himself into furious speed, rushed among the boats with open jaws, and offered battle on every side. Even though harpoons were darted at him from every side, the white whale seemed intent on destroying every boat. But handled like trained chargers in the field, the boats for a while kept out of the way of the fish, though at times by only a plank's breadth. And all the time Ahab's cry could be heard over all others.

But at last the white whale so crossed and recrossed and in a thousand ways entangled the slack of the three lines now fast to him that the boats were drawn close to the whale. For a moment the fish drew aside a little as if to rally for a tremendous charge. Ahab, seizing this opportunity, paid out more line and then was jerking and hauling in upon it again, hoping to untangle some of it, when there was a sight more savage than the fighting teeth of sharks.

With the lines caught and twisted and with loose harpoons and lances flying, Moby Dick charged at

Ahab's boat. There was but one thing to do, and Ahab seized the boat knife and cut the line. That instant the white whale made a sudden rush among the remaining tangles of the other lines, dragging the more entangled boats of Stubb and Flask under the sea as he dived. The two crews, thrown into the water, swam for oars and other floating furniture. Little Flask bobbed up and down like a bottle, twitching his legs to avoid sharks, and Stubb was calling for someone to rescue him.

Ahab's boat, unharmed, was coming to the rescue, when the vessel was sent upward, as if drawn by unseen wires. Like an arrow from the bottom of the sea, the white whale had dashed his broad forehead against the bottom of the boat, and sent it turning over and over into the air until it fell, top downward, and Ahab and his men struggled out from under it like seals from a seaside cave. Then the whale, seeming to feel that his work for the time was done, pushed his forehead through the ocean, and carrying with him the tangled lines, started away at a slow pace.

As before, the ship, having seen the whole fight, again came rushing to the rescue; and dropping a boat, picked up the floating sailors, tubs, oars, and whatever else might be caught and safely landed them upon her decks. There were some sprained shoulders, wrists and ankles, some cuts, bent harpoons and lances, tangled rope, shattered oars, and planks, but no serious ill had come to anyone.

Ahab had been found hanging to the broken half of a boat, but he was not nearly so tired as he had been the day before. But when he was helped to the deck, all eyes were on him. Instead of standing by himself, he half-hung on the shoulder of Starbuck, who had been the first to help him. Ahab's ivory leg had been snapped off, leaving but one short, sharp splinter.

"The band did not hold, sir," said the carpenter, now coming up. "I put good work into that leg."

"No bones broken, sir, I hope," said Stubb.

"Masthead, which way is the white whale going?"

"Away from the ship, sir."

"Up helm, then. Pile on the sail again, shipkeepers. Down the rest of the spare boats and get them ready. Mr. Starbuck, away, and call together the boat's crews."

"Let me first help thee toward the bulwarks, sir."

"Oh, oh, oh! How this splinter hurts me now!"

"Sir?"

"Give me something for a cane—there, that shivered lance will do. Call the men together. But where is Fedallah? Missing? It can not be! Quick! Call all the men together."

What the old man had thought was true, and when the men were counted, Fedallah was not to be found.

"Fedallah!" cried Stubb. "He must have been caught in—"

"Run, all of ye!" shouted Ahab. "Look above, below, cabin, forecastle—find him—not gone—not gone!" But quickly they returned with the news that Fedallah could not be found.

"Yes, sir," said Stubb. "He was caught among the tangles of your line. I thought I saw him dragged under."

"My line? My line? What does that little word mean? But keep watching Moby Dick. Quick! All hands to the rigging of the boats. Collect the oars. Harpooneers, the irons, the irons! Hoist the sails higher. I'll ten times travel the world and dive straight through it, but I'll slay him yet!"

"Never, never, can you capture him, old man!" cried Starbuck. "In Jesus' name, no more of this. That's worse than the devil's madness. Two days you have chased him, and twice you have been beaten into splinters. Thy very leg has been broken. Shall we keep chasing this murderous fish until he kills the last man? Shall we be dragged by him to the bottom of the sea?"

"Starbuck, lately I have felt kindly toward thee, ever since we talked about our wives and our sons. But when it comes to the whale, what you say is not important to me. Two days Moby Dick has floated. Tomorrow will be the third. Yes, men, he'll rise once more, but only to spout his last! D'ye feel brave, men, brave?"

"As fearless fire!" cried Stubb. And when night descended, the whale was still in sight.

So once more the sail was shortened, and everything passed very much the same as it did on the previous night. The sound of hammers and the hum of the grindstone were heard until nearly daylight as the men toiled by lanterns rigging the spare boats and sharpening their fresh weapons for the next day. The carpenter made Ahab another leg, and Ahab, as on the night before, stood watch from his scuttle.

37 The Chase Ends —Third Day

The morning of the third day dawned fair and fresh, and once more the single night man at the front masthead was relieved by crowds of daylight lookouts, who dotted every mast and almost every spar.

"D'ye see him?" cried Ahab. But the whale was not yet in sight. "What a lovely day again! A fairer day could not dawn upon the world. What d'ye see now?"

"Nothing, sir."

"Nothing! And noon is at hand! No one has a claim so far on the gold doubloon! Perhaps I have sailed over Moby Dick. Yes, he's chasing me now, and I'm not chasing him! That's bad. I might have known it, too. The lines and harpoons he's carrying have slowed him down, and I have run by him last night. Turn around! Turn around!"

"Stand by to swing me up!" cried Ahab advancing to the basket. "We should meet him soon."

"Yes, yes, sir." And Starbuck did as he was told, and once more Ahab swung on high.

A whole hour now passed, but at last Ahab found the spout again, and instantly from the three mastheads three shouts called out.

"Face to face, I meet thee, this third time, Moby Dick! He's too far off to lower yet, Mr. Starbuck. He travels fast." Ahab then ordered that he be lowered to the deck, and soon the boats were lowered into the sea.

"Starbuck!" said Ahab.

"Sir?"

"For the third time I start upon this voyage after Moby Dick."

"Aye, sir, but that's the way you wish it."

"Some ships sail from their ports and ever afterwards are missing, Starbuck!"

"Truth, sir, saddest truth."

"I am old. Shake hands with me, man." Their hands met, and tears came from Starbuck's eyes.

"Oh, my captain, my captain! Noble heart. Go not, go not!"

But Ahab only answered, "Lower away! Stand by the crew!" In an instant the boat carrying Ahab was pulling away from the ship.

"The sharks! The sharks!" cried a voice from the cabin window. "O master, my master, come back!" But Ahab heard nothing, and the boat leaped on.

But what the voice said was true, for Ahab's boat had hardly left the ship when numbers of sharks, which seemed to rise from out the dark waters beneath the hull, snapped at the blades of the oars they dipped into the water. Such a thing is not uncommon in those swarming seas.

"Future things swim before me, as in empty skeletons, and all the past is somehow grown dim," Starbuck murmured to himself. "Mary, girl, my wife, I can not see you. My boy, I seem to see only your eyes grown wondrous blue. Is my journey's end coming? My legs feel faint."

The boats had not gone very far, when by a signal from the masthead, a downward-pointed arm, Ahab knew that the whale had gone down. Suddenly the waters around them slowly swelled in broad circles. A low rumbling sound was heard, and all held their breaths as burdened with trailing ropes, harpoons, and lances, a vast form came up from the sea. Covered in a thin veil of mist, the whale hovered for a moment, and then fell back into the deep. The waters flashed for an instant like heaps of fountains and then sank in a shower of flakes, leaving the circling surface creamed like new milk.

"Give way!" cried Ahab to the oarsmen, and the boats darted forward to the attack. But maddened by yesterday's fresh irons that rusted in him, Moby Dick came churning his tail among the boats. Once more he tossed the boats here and there, spilling out the irons and lances from the two mates' boats and damaging them somewhat, but Ahab's boat was left almost without a scar.

While Daggoo and Queequeg were repairing the strained planks, the whale turned and showed one entire side as he shot by them. At that moment a quick cry went up, for among the tangled ropes about the whale was the half-torn body of Fedallah, its eyes turned upon old Ahab.

The harpoon dropped from Ahab's hand. "Away, mates, to the ship! Those boats are useless now. Repair them if you can in time, and return to me. If not, Ahab can die! Down, men, I will harpoon the first man that offers to jump from the boat I stand in. Ye are not other men, but my arms and my legs, and so obey me. Where's the whale? Gone down again?"

As if escaping with the corpse he bore, Moby Dick was now again steadily swimming forward, and had almost passed the ship, which had been sailing toward him on this third day. He seemed to be swimming as fast as he could, taking his own straight path in the sea.

"Old Ahab," cried Starbuck, "it's not too late, even

now, the third day, to stop! See! Moby Dick seeks thee not. It is thou that madly seekest him!"

At last Ahab's boat was sliding by the ship, and Ahab called to Starbuck to turn the vessel around and follow him, but not too swiftly. Glancing upward, Ahab saw Tashtego, Queequeg, and Daggoo eagerly mounting the mastheads. The oarsmen were busy repairing the two staved boats, which had just been hoisted to the side. One after the other, through the portholes, as he sped, he caught flying glimpses of Stubb and Flask busying themselves on deck among bundles of new irons and lances. And now seeing that the flag was gone from the main masthead, Ahab ordered Tashtego to place another one there.

It might have been because of the three days' running chase, or it might have been the hatred in him, but the whale was not traveling so fast as he once had been. And as Ahab glided over the waves, the sharks still kept after him. So close did they stick to the boat and so continually bite at the oars, that the blades became jagged and left splinters in the sea at almost every dip.

"Heed them not! Pull on!"

"But at every bite, sir, the thin blades grow smaller and smaller!"

"They will last long enough! Pull on! But who can tell," he muttered, "whether these sharks swim to feast on a whale or on Ahab? But pull on! All alive now—we near him. The helm! Take the helm! Let me pass!" And so saying, Ahab went forward to the bows in the still flying boat.

At length the boat came close to the whale, so close that Ahab was within the smoky mountain mist thrown off from the whale's spout. He was even so close to him that he was able to dart his fierce iron into the hated whale. As the steel hit Moby Dick, he turned sideways, rolled his flank against the boat, and without staving a hole in it, rolled the boat over. Had it not been for the elevated part of the gunwale to which he then clung, Ahab would have been tossed into the sea. As it was, three of the oarsmen were flung out, two of them managing to hang to the gunwale and finally to get aboard again. The third was thrown helplessly astern, but still afloat and swimming.

Then, with great swiftness, the white whale darted through the sea, and Ahab shouted to the steersman to hold the line. But the line, placed under such a strain, would not hold, and it snapped in the empty air. "Oars, oars, burst in upon him!" cried Ahab.

Hearing the rush of the boat, the whale wheeled around and caught sight of the ship. Seeming to think the ship was the cause of all his trouble, the whale all of a sudden bore down upon its advancing prow, smiting his jaws amid fiery showers of foam.

Ahab staggered; his hand struck his forehead. "I grow blind. Hands! Stretch out before me that I may find my way."

"The whale! The ship!" cried the oarsmen.

"Oars! Oars! Dash on, my men! Will ye not save my ship?" As the oarsmen forced their boat through the sea, the two damaged planks let so much water through that the craft was nearly level with the waves. Its half-wading, splashing crew tried hard to stop the gap and bail out the pouring water.

As Tashtego had gone up to replace the flag, he caught sight of the oncoming monster, as did Starbuck and Stubb, who were standing on the deck.

"The whale, the whale!" cried Stubb. "Up helm, up helm! Let not Starbuck die! Up helm, I say—ye fools,

the jaw! The jaw! Is this the end of all my prayers? The whale turns to meet us. My God, stand by me now!"

"Oh, Stubb," said Flask, "I hope my mother has drawn my part-pay before this time. If not, a few coppers will come to her now, for the voyage is up."

From the ship's bows nearly all of the men now hung, with hammers, bits of planks, lances, and harpoons in their hands, just as they had come from their jobs. All of their eyes were upon the whale, which sent a broad band of overspreading foam before him as he rushed. And in spite of all that the men could do, the solid white of his forehead smote the ship's right bow and the men and timbers reeled. Some fell flat upon their faces, as through the break in the ship the water poured like a mountain stream.

Diving beneath the settling ship, the whale ran along its keel. But turning under water, he swiftly shot to the surface again, within a few yards of Ahab's boat.

"Toward thee I roll," cried Ahab, "thou all-destroying but unconquering whale! To the last I shall fight thee. I stab at thee, and for hate's sake I spite my last breath at thee. *Thus*, take this spear."

The harpoon was darted, and the stricken whale flew forward. When the line became entangled, Ahab stopped to clear it, but as he did so, a turn caught him round the neck. And before the crew knew it, he was shot out of the boat and gone. Next instant, the rope's final end flew out of the tub, knocked down an oarsman, and striking the sea, disappeared into the depths.

For a moment the boat's crew stood still. Then they turned. "The ship? Great God, where is the ship?" Soon they saw only the uppermost masts out of the water, and the pagan harpooneers still kept their sinking lookouts on the sea. Whirling waters seized the lone boat itself, and all its crew, each floating oar, and every lance pole were carried down into the sea. Soon the *Pequod* could be seen no more.

And the great sea rolled on as it rolled five thousand years ago.

38   *The Story is Finished*

After Fedallah's disappearance, I was ordered to take his place as Ahab's bowman. And on that last day, when the men were thrown out, the upset boat tossed me far to the rear. After the boat, the ship, and all the other men had slipped into the sea, the coffin lifebuoy shot up from the sea, and I was kept afloat. Buoyed up by that coffin for almost one whole day and night, I somehow was left unharmed by the sharks and sea hawks. On the second day, a ship drew nearer and nearer and picked me up at last. It was the *Rachel*, who, still hunting her missing children, had found only me, another orphan.

The End

REVIEWING YOUR READING

CHAPTER 1

FINDING THE MAIN IDEA

1. In this chapter the author is mostly interested in
(A) teaching us about whales   (B) introducing us to
Ishmael   (C) describing a cheap inn   (D) telling us about
the South Seas

REMEMBERING DETAIL

2. When Ishmael goes to sea, he goes as a
(A) simple sailor   (B) passenger   (C) cook   (D) captain
3. The main reason Ishmael wanted to go on a whaling voyage
was to
(A) earn some money   (B) get wholesome exercise
(C) see a whale   (D) be with his friends

DRAWING CONCLUSIONS

4. You can tell from the story so far that Ishmael is
(A) self-righteous   (B) kind   (C) skillful
(D) adventurous

USING YOUR REASON

5. When the landlord said "if you are goin' a-whalin', you'd
better get used to that sort of thing" (sharing a bed), he
meant that
(A) harpooneers are dangerous   (B) there are no beds on
whaling ships   (C) Ishmael was lucky to get a bed at all
(D) life on a whaling ship is rough

READING FOR DEEPER MEANING

6. The author would most agree with which of the following?
(A) Honesty is the best policy.   (B) You can't judge a
book by its cover.   (C) Let sleeping dogs lie.   (D) Blood
is thicker than water.

THINKING IT OVER

1. Why did Ishmael want to go to sea? Do you feel the same way
he does about the sea? Explain.
2. On the basis of what you have read so far, do you think that
you would like to change places with Ishmael? Give reasons
for your choice.

229

CHAPTER 2

FINDING THE MAIN IDEA

1. In this chapter the author is mostly interested in
   (A) telling more about Ishmael and Queequeg
   (B) describing New Bedford   (C) telling what the whalers
   had for breakfast   (D) describing the way in which
   Queequeg shaved

DRAWING CONCLUSIONS

2. You can guess from the story that Queequeg
   (A) does not understand or speak English very well
   (B) never listens to what people are saying   (C) is deaf
   (D) is stupid

3. Queequeg shaved with his harpoon because
   (A) it was dangerous   (B) he was in a hurry   (C) it was
   very sharp   (D) he wanted to surprise Ishmael

USING YOUR REASON

4. Instead of saying "a man like Queequeg you don't see every
   day" the author would have meant the same thing if he had
   said that Queequeg
   (A) is a fine man   (B) would make a good friend   (C) is a
   very unusual man   (D) is pretty ordinary

5. When the author says "his (Queequeg's) greatest admirer
   could hardly have justified bringing his harpoon to
   breakfast with him" he meant
   (A) Queequeg's table manners are bad   (B) Queequeg has
   many admirers   (C) nobody likes Queequeg
   (D) Queequeg is greedy

READING FOR DEEPER MEANING

6. The author seems to think that when people play tricks on
   you the thing to do is to
   (A) be very angry with them   (B) play a trick on them in
   return   (C) demand an explanation   (D) take it in good
   part

THINKING IT OVER

1. What do you think about the following: "Say what you will, it
   is marvelous how polite these savages are"? Explain.

2. In what ways is Queequeg unusual?

CHAPTER 3

FINDING THE MAIN IDEA

1. This chapter is mostly about Father Mapple's
   (A) childhood   (B) sermon   (C) congregation
   (D) personal appearance

REMEMBERING DETAIL

2. Ishmael's jacket was made of
   (A) wool   (B) cotton   (C) bearskin   (D) silk
3. After Jonah was dropped into the water he
   (A) sank to the bottom   (B) was swallowed by a whale
   (C) drowned   (D) was swept away by a strong current

USING YOUR REASON

4. You can tell from this chapter that Ishmael is
   (A) foolish   (B) pessimistic   (C) sentimental
   (D) optimistic
5. When the author said "Father Mapple was in the hardy winter
   of a healthy old age" he meant that Father Mapple
   (A) was very frail   (B) was not as old as Ishmael
   (C) although very old was also very healthy   (D) was not
   very old

IDENTIFYING THE MOOD

6. When Ishmael first read the marble tablets in the chapel he
   felt
   (A) merry   (B) bored   (C) depressed   (D) confident

READING FOR DEEPER MEANING

7. Father Mapple's sermon was really about
   (A) the creation of man   (B) life eternal   (C) love and
   joy   (D) sin and repentance

THINKING IT OVER

1. What about the chapel showed that there is danger and grief
   in whaling? If there was an activity you particularly wanted
   to take part in, how would the possibility of danger affect
   your feelings about the activity?
2. During Father Mapple's sermon a great storm was blowing
   outside the chapel. What effect, if any, do you think the storm
   had on how the listeners felt?

CHAPTER 4

FINDING THE MAIN IDEA

1. This chapter is mainly about
   (A) Queequeg   (B) Christians   (C) pagans   (D) canoes

REMEMBERING DETAIL

2. Queequeg's father was a
   (A) seaman   (B) high priest   (C) warrior   (D) king
3. Queequeg's reason for leaving his native island was to
   (A) travel   (B) get away from his father   (C) learn from
   the Christians   (D) learn another language

DRAWING CONCLUSIONS

4. You can tell that, after some time among the whalers,
   Queequeg's feeling about Christians was one of
   (A) joy   (B) disappointment   (C) happiness
   (D) excitement
5. Ishmael's purpose in joining with Queequeg to worship the
   idol was to
   (A) please Queequeg   (B) experience something new
   (C) deceive Queequeg   (D) get Queequeg to join with him
   in Presbyterian worship

THINKING IT OVER

1. Do you think that you would have been drawn to Queequeg
   as Ishmael was? Why or why not?
2. On the basis of what you have read so far, would you like to
   change places with Queequeg? Explain.
3. If you were Ishmael, would you have joined with Queequeg
   in worshipping his idol? Explain.

CHAPTER 5

FINDING THE MAIN IDEA

1. In this chapter the author is mainly interested in telling us
   about the character of
   (A) Ishmael   (B) Mrs. Hussey   (C) Queequeg
   (D) Queequeg's father

REMEMBERING DETAIL

2. What did Queequeg do to the young man who annoyed him?

(A) Threw him overboard (B) Hit him with his harpoon
(C) Threw him up in the air (D) Threw him down the
stairs

3. After first being angry with Queequeg, the captain begged his
pardon because
(A) he was afraid of Queequeg (B) Ishmael threatened to
beat him (C) Queequeg saved the young man's life
(D) he realized that Queequeg had reason to be annoyed

DRAWING CONCLUSIONS

4. You can tell from this chapter that Queequeg is
(A) slow-witted (B) unfair (C) pompous
(D) quick-witted

5. Queequeg rescued the young man who went overboard
because
(A) the captain told him to (B) it seemed to be the natural
thing to do (C) he felt like going for a swim (D) he
wanted to show up the other passengers

USING YOUR REASON

6. Instead of saying that Queequeg did not seem "to think he
deserved all the honor," the author would have meant the
same thing if he had said that Queequeg was very
(A) modest (B) arrogant (C) friendly
(D) self-satisfied

THINKING IT OVER

1. Why did the captain of the merchant ship wash his hands
in the punch bowl? Why did Queequeg's people laugh at
him? People from many different nations are living in this
country today. Do you think that similar misunderstandings
are likely to arise among them? Have you ever been in such
a situation? Explain.

CHAPTER 6

FINDING THE MAIN IDEA

1. In this chapter the author is mostly interested in
(A) telling us how Captain Ahab lost his leg
(B) describing the lay system (C) introducing us to the
Pequod and Captain Ahab (D) explaining about Ramadan

REMEMBERING DETAIL

2. While Ishmael chose a whaling ship Queequeg stayed at the inn because he was
(A) tired and wanted to sleep   (B) observing Ramadan
(C) eating breakfast   (D) working on his harpoon

IDENTIFYING THE MOOD

3. Which of the following best describes Captain Peleg's feelings about the merchant service?
(A) It's better than whaling.   (B) It's not as good as whaling.   (C) It's as good as whaling.   (D) He does not know anything about it.

DRAWING CONCLUSIONS

4. In this chapter we begin to get the feeling that
(A) there is some reason to think Ishmael will not enjoy whaling   (B) Queequeg does not really want to go whaling
(C) Ishmael and Queequeg will not stay friends   (D) there is some mystery about Captain Ahab that will affect Queequeg and Ishmael

5. Which of the following best describes Queequeg's relationship with Ishmael?
(A) Excitement   (B) Gaiety   (C) Trust   (C) Pride

THINKING IT OVER

1. If you were Ishmael, would you have made sure of seeing Captain Ahab before you signed on for three years? Explain.

2. If you were Ishmael, would you still have wanted to go whaling after talking to Peleg? Explain.

CHAPTER 7

FINDING THE MAIN IDEA

1. This chapter is mostly about
(A) Ishmael's religion   (B) Mrs. Hussey's inn   (C) the *Pequod*   (D) Queequeg's Ramadan

DRAWING CONCLUSIONS

2. You can tell from this chapter that Queequeg
(A) believes that Chiristianity is better than his own religion
(B) takes his religion seriously   (C) has no feelings about religion   (D) does not take his religion seriously

234

3. After the Ramadan, Ishmael talked to Queequeg about religion because
(A) he wanted to persuade him that there were other, better religions　(B) he liked to talk about religion　(C) Queequeg asked him to　(D) he wanted to learn more about Queequeg's religion

IDENTIFYING THE MOOD

4. Which of the following best describes how Ishmael felt when he could not get into Queequeg's room?
(A) Surprised　(B) Afraid　(C) Annoyed　(D) Glad

THINKING IT OVER

1. Ishmael has always claimed to be tolerant about religion. Why, then, does he "argue the point" with Queequeg after the Ramadan? Do you think that Ishmael really believes that other religions are as good as his own? Explain.

CHAPTER 8

FINDING THE MAIN IDEA

1. In this chapter the author is mainly interested in
(A) describing Elijah　(B) describing how to throw a harpoon　(C) showing how good Queequeg is with a harpoon　(D) planting the idea that the voyage may not be an ordinary one

REMEMBERING DETAIL

2. At first Bildad, and Peleg did not want Queequeg aboard because
(A) he was a cannibal　(B) they didn't need him　(C) he was too big　(D) they had never met him before
3. Bildad and Peleg later want Queequeg to sign on because
(A) they liked his looks　(B) he told them that he was an experienced harpooneer　(C) he showed them how good he was with a harpoon　(D) Ishmael refused to go unless they signed on Queequeg

DRAWING CONCLUSIONS

4. You can tell from this chapter that Bildad is
(A) proud　(B) greedy　(C) religious　(D) brave

5. Queequeg threw his harpoon because
(A) he wanted to frighten Peleg and Bildad   (B) it was
the best way to show how well he could use it   (C) he
needed the practice   (D) it slipped from his hand

THINKING IT OVER

1. What is the author's purpose in bringing Elijah into the
story? Explain your answer.

CHAPTER 9

FINDING THE MAIN IDEA

1. This chapter is mostly about
(A) Charity Bildad   (B) the preparation of a whaling ship
for a long voyage   (C) manning the capstan   (D) the
Atlantic Ocean in winter

REMEMBERING DETAIL

2. When Queequeg and Ishmael came to the wharf early on the
morning of their departure, Ishmael thought he saw
(A) Charity   (B) Peleg   (C) sailors   (D) shadows

DRAWING CONCLUSIONS

3. You can tell that Peleg and Bildad
(A) would like to have stayed on board   (B) were glad to
go back to port   (C) do not like the sea   (D) are not
good seamen

4. It took so long to get the *Pequod* ready to sail because
(A) the workers were slow   (B) there was so much to be
done   (C) Peleg and Bildad were no good at the job
(D) Captain Ahab's absence made things difficult

IDENTIFYING THE MOOD

5. How did Ishmael feel about not having seen Ahab yet?
(A) Pleased   (B) Happy   (C) Unhappy   (D) Indifferent

THINKING IT OVER

1. Can you see any similarity between the preparations needed
for a whaling voyage, as described by Ishmael, and the
preparations needed for a voyage into space today? Explain.

2. If you were Ishmael, would you have sailed with the *Pequod*
after Elijah's warnings? Would you first have tried to find out
more about Captain Ahab? Elijah? Explain.

CHAPTER 10

THINKING IT OVER

1. Look up *whale* in an encyclopedia. Does the description of whales agree with the author's? What characteristics of whales does the author seem to admire? Why do you think he admires them?

CHAPTER 11

REMEMBERING DETAIL

1. Starbuck was
   (A) fearless   (B) cowardly   (C) careless
   (D) superstitious
2. Stubb was
   (A) brave   (B) easygoing   (C) mean   (D) cowardly
3. Queequeg was harpooneer for
   (A) Stubb   (B) Starbuck   (C) Flask   (D) Tashtego

DRAWING CONCLUSIONS

4. You can tell from this chapter that
   (A) Starbuck will end up disagreeing with Ahab
   (B) Starbuck does not like Stubb   (C) Queequeg is popular with the crew   (D) Ishmael does not like any of the mates
5. Queequeg is probably Starbuck's harpooneer because
   (A) he asked to be   (B) Starbuck, as chief mate, had first choice and thought Queequeg was best   (C) Stubb did not want him   (D) Flask did not want him

THINKING IT OVER

1. What did Starbuck mean when he said "I will have no man in my boat who is not afraid of a whale"? Do you agree with him? Explain.

CHAPTER 12

FINDING THE MAIN IDEA

1. This chapter is mostly about
   (A) Stubb   (B) Captain Ahab   (C) Flask   (D) the cook

REMEMBERING DETAIL

2. Ahab's artificial leg was made from
   (A) a piece of wood   (B) plastic   (C) the jaw of a whale
   (D) metal

3. Ahab was angry at Stubb for
   (A) not doing his job properly   (B) being rude to him
   (C) getting in his way   (D) suggesting that Ahab pad the
   end of his leg

4. Ahab wanted the sailors to keep their eyes open for a
   (A) sperm whale   (B) white whale   (C) killer whale
   (D) narwhal

DRAWING CONCLUSIONS

5. You can tell from this chapter that there is some mystery
   connected with
   (A) the after hold   (B) the weather   (C) Stubb
   (D) Ishmael

USING YOUR REASON

6. When Ahab said, "What business have I with this pipe? This
   thing is meant for quietness. I'll smoke no more" he would
   have meant the same thing if he had said
   (A) I've got too much to do to waste time smoking   (B) my
   mind is not quiet and at rest   (C) I don't like this tobacco
   (D) smoking makes me sleepy

IDENTIFYING THE MOOD

7. Which of the following best describes Stubb's feelings about
   Ahab?
   (A) Respect   (B) Mistrust   (C) Anger   (D) Trust

READING FOR DEEPER MEANING

8. It is becoming more and more obvious that Captain Ahab is
   a man with
   (A) something on his mind   (B) a kindly face   (C) an
   even temper   (D) a very ordinary attitude

THINKING IT OVER

1. What are your impressions of Captain Ahab so far? Would
   you like to be a member of his crew? Explain.

2. What hints does the author give in this chapter that some
   kind of drama is to take place?

238

3. What do you make of Stubb's dream and his interpretation of it?

CHAPTER 13

FINDING THE MAIN IDEA

1. In this chapter the author is mostly interested in telling us about
(A) Dough-Boy   (B) the kind of food whalers eat
(C) the cabin and how it is used   (D) the harpooneers' table manners

REMEMBERING DETAIL

2. Who dined in the captain's cabin after Ahab and the mates?
(A) The steward   (B) The Crew   (C) The cook
(D) The Harpooneers

3. To satisfy the harpooneers' hunger, Dough-Boy would bring out
(A) spices   (B) old-fashioned beef   (C) a hunk of solid ox   (D) salt

DRAWING CONCLUSIONS

4. You can tell from this chapter that the mates
(A) would like to spend more time in the cabin   (B) were glad they did not have to spend any more time in the cabin
(C) looked forward to their meals   (D) were unhappy when dinner came to an end

5. The mates dined with Captain Ahab because
(A) they liked to   (B) it was the custom   (C) they were served better food at the captain's table   (D) there was nowhere else for them to go

IDENTIFYING THE MOOD

6. Which of the following best describes how the three mates feel as they dine with Ahab?
(A) Comfortable   (B) Uncomfortable   (C) Happy
(D) Honored

THINKING IT OVER

1. What does dinner in the cabin show about the relationship between Ahab and the mates? Explain your answer.

CHAPTER 14

FINDING THE MAIN IDEA

1. The main aim of this chapter is to
   (A) describe Moby Dick   (B) reveal the real purpose of the voyage for Ahab   (C) describe the crew   (D) describe life on board ship

REMEMBERING DETAIL

2. Only one man opposed Ahab's plan to track down Moby Dick. He was
   (A) Ishmael   (B) Queequeg   (C) Stubb   (D) Starbuck

DRAWING CONCLUSIONS

3. You can tell from this chapter that the hunt for Moby Dick will probably
   (A) be a long one   (B) end in disaster   (C) be boring
   (D) be successful

USING YOUR REASON

4. When the harpooneer said "Whales are as scarce as hen's teeth whenever thou are up there" he meant that Ishmael
   (A) frightened off the whales   (B) was a good lookout
   (C) did not keep a proper lookout   (D) could not see any whales because there weren't any

5. Ahab is determined to hunt down Moby Dick because
   (A) he is obsessed with the idea of getting revenge   (B) they will get a lot of oil from Moby Dick   (C) the ship's owners told him to capture Moby Dick   (D) he wants to annoy Starbuck

IDENTIFYING THE MOOD

6. When Ahab made it clear that he was going to hunt down Moby Dick, Starbuck was
   (A) surprised   (B) glad   (C) angry   (D) afraid

THINKING IT OVER

1. Do you agree with Starbuck that "Revenge on a dumb brute" is madness? Explain.
2. How would you feel about Ahab's desire to hunt down Moby Dick if you were a member of his crew?

CHAPTER 15

FINDING THE MAIN IDEA

1. The author's main purpose in this chapter is to
(A) show us how Ishmael feels about Moby Dick   (B) tell
us more about Moby Dick   (C) describe the traveling habits
of the sperm whale   (D) describe how whales sometimes
damage ships

REMEMBERING DETAIL

2. Archy thought he heard
(A) a whale   (B) the hum of the keel   (C) a cough
(D) the flapping of a sail

DRAWING CONCLUSIONS

3. There is a hint in this chapter that
(A) Ishmael will fight Moby Dick and win   (B) the crew
will turn against Captain Ahab   (C) Captain Ahab will
defeat Moby Dick   (D) there are some people in the after
hold who are not part of the regular crew
4. Ahab spent so much time on his charts because he
(A) was marking the ship's route on them   (B) was working
out the best places to look for Moby Dick   (C) believed it
was part of his job as captain   (D) had nothing better to do
with his time

IDENTIFYING THE MOOD

5. What Ishmael has learned about Moby Dick must have made
him feel
(A) admiring   (B) curious   (C) afraid   (D) anxious to
see him

USING YOUR REASON

6. It has become clear by now, at least to Ishmael, that Captain
Ahab is
(A) mad   (B) sane   (C) cowardly   (D) clear-headed

THINKING IT OVER

1. Have your ideas about whaling changed in any way as you
have read from the first chapter in the book to this one?
Explain.

2. Earlier on, you were asked if you would like to change places with Ishmael. Would you give the same answer now? Explain.

CHAPTER 16

FINDING THE MAIN IDEA

1. The author's main purpose in this chapter is to
(A) describe a storm at sea   (B) show just how mad Ahab is   (C) show how the crew feels about Ahab   (D) describe a whale hunt

REMEMBERING DETAIL

2. When the first whale was sighted, Captain Ahab brought out
(A) five stowaways   (B) rum for all the sailors   (C) extra harpoons   (D) a new pipe for Stubb

DRAWING CONCLUSIONS

3. You can tell from this chapter that Ishmael now realizes how
(A) careful a whaler Starbuck is   (B) dangerous this voyage is likely to be   (C) skillful Queequeg is   (D) cruel Stubb is

4. Ahab pretended that this voyage was no different from any other because he
(A) wanted to catch as many whales as possible   (B) was afraid that the crew might turn against him   (C) was told to do so by Starbuck   (D) wanted to convince himself that it was no different

IDENTIFYING THE MOOD

5. Which of the following best describes Starbuck's feelings when the five stowaways appear?
(A) Resignation   (B) Fury   (C) Pleasure
(D) Indifference

THINKING IT OVER

1. Were you surprised when the five stowaways suddenly appeared? Why had Ahab brought them on board? Explain.

2. Do you agree with Ishmael that "of all tools used, men are most likely to get out of order"? Explain.

CHAPTER 17

FINDING THE MAIN IDEA

1. This chapter is mostly about
   (A) Moby Dick (B) Starbuck (C) the Cape of Good
   Hope (D) the journey of the *Pequod*

USING YOUR REASON

2. Instead of saying, "Cape of Good Hope, do they call ye?"
   Ishmael would have meant the same thing if he had said
   (A) Cape of Good Hope is a good name (B) I like that
   name (C) I wonder who named it such? (D) Cape of
   Good Hope is not a good name

3. Ahab had hidden five extra men in the after hold because
   (A) the owners of the *Pequod* were too mean to supply him
   with all the crew he needed (B) he knew the owners would
   not approve of his joining in the whale hunt with his own
   boat (C) there was no room for them in the crew's
   quarters (D) he did not want them to have to do any
   ordinary work

READING FOR DEEPER MEANING

4. It is clear from this chapter that Ahab is
   (A) still obsessed with the idea of hunting down Moby
   Dick (B) getting tired of the chase (C) bored
   (D) feeling ill

THINKING IT OVER

1. Do you think that Ahab's plan to join personally in the hunt
   for Moby Dick is wise? Explain.

CHAPTER 18

REMEMBERING DETAIL

1. The first ship to give Ahab news of Moby Dick was the
   (A) *Town-Ho* (B) *Albatross* (C) *Goney* (D) *Pequod*

2. A gam is a
   (A) barrel of oil (B) whale (C) ship's sail (D) social
   meeting of whale ships

DRAWING CONCLUSIONS

3. You can tell from this chapter that Ahab is determined to
(A) ignore all other whaling ships   (B) capture Moby Dick
or die in the attempt   (C) meet with the captain of every
whaling ship sighted   (D) capture Moby Dick and tow him
to Nantucket

IDENTIFYING THE MOOD

4. How do you think that Ishmael felt after hearing the latest
news of Moby Dick?
(A) Thrilled   (B) Unafraid   (C) Surprised   (D) Afraid

THINKING IT OVER

1. Why are whaling ships happy to meet other whaling ships
at sea?

CHAPTER 19

FINDING THE MAIN IDEA

1. The author's main purpose in this chapter is to
(A) describe brit   (B) describe the feeding habits of sperm
whales   (C) warn us that the *Pequod* may never return to
port   (D) describe the great live squid

REMEMBERING DETAIL

2. Daggoo saw
(A) Moby Dick   (B) a mass of brit   (C) Java   (D) the
great live squid

USING YOUR REASON

3. Starbuck would almost rather have fought Moby Dick than
seen the great live squid because he
(A) does not like the look of the squid   (B) knows the
superstition about the squid   (C) thinks that the squid
will kill them all   (D) thinks that Moby Dick would be
easier to fight

IDENTIFYING THE MOOD

4. After hearing from Starbuck about the great live squid, the
crew feels
(A) confidence   (B) sadness   (C) anger   (D) fear

244

THINKING IT OVER

1. If you were Ishmael, how would you feel after hearing Starbuck's explanation of the great live squid? How would you feel about changing places with Ishmael now?

2. Why does the author bring the superstition about the great live squid into the story? Does it create any kind of mood? Explain.

CHAPTER 20

FINDING THE MAIN IDEA

1. This chapter is about
   (A) Stubb   (B) the killing of a whale   (C) whale meat
   (D) sharks

REMEMBERING DETAIL

2. "There go flukes" means
   (A) the whale is going underwater   (B) the whale is dead
   (C) there is a whale in sight   (D) sharks are feasting on the whale

3. The first member of the crew to kill a whale was
   (A) Queequeg   (B) Ahab   (C) Tashtego   (D) Stubb

DRAWING CONCLUSIONS

4. You can tell from this chapter that Ahab
   (A) has lost interest in catching Moby Dick   (B) still wants to catch Moby Dick   (C) finds whaling dull   (D) wants to go home

USING YOUR REASON

5. When the author says "The boat now flew through the water like a shark which was all fins" he meant the boat was
   (A) going very fast   (B) clumsy   (C) comfortable
   (D) in danger of overturning

IDENTIFYING THE MOOD

6. As the boats chased the whales, the harpooneers were
   (A) very bored   (B) fearful   (C) calm   (D) wildly excited

THINKING IT OVER

1. When the whale finally dies, Stubb says "Yes; both pipes smoked out!" What does he mean? Why does he use this expression?

CHAPTER 21

FINDING THE MAIN IDEA

1. The main purpose of this chapter is to
(A) describe the butchering of a whale   (B) show how
sharks are kept away from the dead whale   (C) describe the
hunting of a right whale   (D) describe the meeting with the
Jeroboam

DRAWING CONCLUSIONS

2. You can tell from this chapter that Fedallah will
(A) be pushed overboard by Stubb   (B) bring bad luck to
the *Pequod*   (C) kill Moby Dick himself   (D) rob Ahab of
his silver watch
3. You can tell that Stubb and Flask
(A) distrust Fedallah   (B) like Fedallah   (C) would like
to be friends with Fedallah   (D) think that Fedallah will
bring the ship good luck

USING YOUR REASON

4. When the author says "You would have thought we were
offering up ten thousand red oxen to the sea gods" he meant
(A) there was blood everywhere   (B) sailors usually
sacrifice to the sea gods   (C) there were live oxen on board
the ship   (D) whales and oxen look alike
5. Ahab wanted a right whale caught because
(A) right whales give a lot of oil   (B) he wanted a whale
steak   (C) he believed that a ship with a sperm whale head
and a right whale head would never sink
(D) he wanted some lard

IDENTIFYING THE MOOD

6. In this chapter we more and more get the feeling that the
Pequod will
(A) be successful   (B) come to some terrible end   (C) get
back to Nantucket safely   (D) kill Moby Dick

THINKING IT OVER

1. Earlier, you were asked if you would like to change places
with Queequeg. Would you give the same answer now?
Explain.

CHAPTER 22

FINDING THE MAIN IDEA
1. The main purpose of this chapter is to describe how
   (A) Queequeg rescued Tashtego   (B) Tashtego found the
   sperm sac   (C) Tashtego fell into the sperm sac
   (D) sperm oil is brought on board

USING YOUR REASON
2. Tashtego rammed the bucket down into the sac
   (A) by mistake   (B) to stop Tashtego from climbing out
   (C) so he could climb down into the sac   (D) because he
   thought Tashtego could grab hold of it and pull himself out

IDENTIFYING THE MOOD
3. What is the quality that Queequeg is always showing?
   (A) cleverness   (B) virtue   (C) humor   (D) courage
4. When the whale's head started to fall into the sea, those
   watching were
   (A) startled   (B) amused   (C) horrified   (D) pleased

THINKING IT OVER
1. Describe the character of Queequeg as you see it. Tell what
   you admire about him and what you dislike about him.

CHAPTER 23

FINDING THE MAIN IDEA
1. This chapter is about
   (A) the *Jungfrau*   (B) the race for a whale   (C) the
   sinking of a recently killed whale   (D) a scarcity of oil

REMEMBERING DETAIL
2. The German captain would have won the race but
   (A) the *Pequod*'s seamen were more skillful   (B) the
   Pequod's mates tricked him   (C) one of his crew made a
   bad stroke in rowing   (D) the whale changed direction
3. Captain de Deer did not stop to put his lamp and oil on board
   the *Jungfrau* because
   (A) he saw whales   (B) he decided to stay on board the
   Pequod   (C) his crew would not let him   (D) he decided
   to go rowing instead

USING YOUR REASON

4. When Stubb said "here's grass growing in the boat's bottom" he really meant

(A) we're going too fast   (B) we're going much too slowly
(C) sometimes plants and grass grow in the bottoms of boats
(D) soon there won't be room for us in the boat

5. In this chapter Flask shows himself to be

(A) the most skillful of the mates   (B) clumsy   (C) cruel
(D) kind-hearted

READING FOR DEEPER MEANING

6. In this chapter the author, or at least Ishmael, seems to be saying that whale hunting is

(A) good sport   (B) boring   (C) exciting   (D) cruel

THINKING IT OVER

1. What happens in this chapter that shows Flask to be cruel?

2. Discuss Stubb's sense of humor. Is his the kind of humor that you enjoy? Explain.

3. Do you get any feeling in this chapter that Ishmael's feelings about whales have changed? Explain.

CHAPTER 24

FINDING THE MAIN IDEA

1. This chapter is mostly about

(A) the pirates   (B) the behavior of whales in herds
(C) drugging   (D) whaling laws

REMEMBERING DETAIL

2. The *Pequod* met the herd of whales

(A) by the Philippine Islands   (B) at the equator   (C) in the Straits of Sunda   (D) in Peru

3. The drugg was used when

(A) the whalers were feeling lazy   (B) all the harpoons had been used   (C) there were too many whales to deal with at once   (D) the weather was bad

USING YOUR REASON

4. The whalers prefer old Nantucket water to fresh water from Peruvian or Indian streams because they

248

(A) do not like leaving the ship to get fresh water   (B) do not like the taste of fresh water   (C) have not the time to collect fresh water   (D) know that the Nantucket water is safe

5. The whales were hurrying through the narrow waters because they
(A) knew that they could easily be caught there   (B) liked to swim fast   (C) were afraid of the pirates   (D) knew the food was better in the open sea

THINKING IT OVER
1. Whose side are you on—the whales or the whalers? Why?
2. What do you think of the author's imagery in this chapter? Do you think that it is successful in creating the picture that he wants? Explain.

CHAPTER 25

FINDING THE MAIN IDEA
1. This chapter is mostly about
(A) ambergris   (B) the trick Stubb played on the captain of the *Rosebud*   (C) blasted whales   (D) how Pip lost his mind

REMEMBERING DETAIL
2. Stubb wanted the dried-up whale because
(A) he knew that it would give good oil   (B) he was very fond of whale steak   (C) he was in the mood for playing tricks   (D) there was the chance that it would contain ambergris

3. Stubb made two trips to the *Rosebud* because
(A) it was a beautiful day   (B) Ahab wanted news of Moby Dick and Stubb did not want to keep him waiting   (C) the *Rosebud*'s mate invited him to come back   (D) the first time he went he forgot part of his business

USING YOUR REASON
4. When Stubb said to the *Rosebud*'s first mate "What's the matter with your nose, there?" he meant
(A) you look as though you have broken your nose
(B) what an ugly nose you have   (C) how on earth can you

stand the smell of that blasted whale? (D) you have a
pimple on your nose

5. The French captain decided to get rid of the whales because
(A) the chief mate told him that Stubb said they were
dangerous to the crew's health (B) Stubb told him that
they would give no oil (C) Stubb told him that they would
drag the ship down (D) he decided they were slowing the
ship down too much

IDENTIFYING THE MOOD

6. How do you think Stubb felt when he found the ambergris?
(A) Dissappointed (B) Amused (C) Surprised
(D) Triumphant

THINKING IT OVER

1. Was Stubb completely honest with the French captain? In the
circumstances, would you have done the same thing?

2. Why do you think that the author casually tosses in the story
of Pip?

CHAPTER 26

FINDING THE MAIN IDEA

1. The main purpose of this chapter is to
(A) describe the English captain (B) show how another
of Moby Dick's victims felt about the whale (C) show how
hard it is for Ahab to get around (D) describe a ship's
surgeon

REMEMBERING DETAIL

2. The English captain had lost his
(A) arm (B) left leg (C) hand D) right foot

3. The English captain's arm was torn by
(A) Moby Dick's teeth (B) a knife (C) a rope (D) the
barb of a harpoon

DRAWING CONCLUSIONS

4. You can tell that the English captain thinks that anyone who
has lost a limb to Moby Dick and want to fight him again is
(A) a fool (B) very brave (C) wise (D) a coward

USING YOUR REASON

5. Instead of saying "This man's blood is at the boiling point"

the surgeon would have meant the same thing if he had said
(A) he seems to have a headache   (B) his brain must have
been affected or he would not want to chase Moby Dick
(C) he is coming down with a cold   (D) this hot weather
does not suit him

6. The English captain will not try to capture Moby Dick again
because
(A) the whale will not give any oil   (B) he thinks it would
be a shame to kill such a noble whale   (C) he does not want
to lose another limb   (D) there would be no glory in killing
him

THINKING IT OVER

1. Compare Ahab's attitude toward Moby Dick with that of the
English captain. Which, do you think, would have been your
attitude if you had ever come into contact with the whale?
Explain.

CHAPTER 27

FINDING THE MAIN IDEA

1. The main purpose of this chapter is to
(A) explain what "up Burtons" means   (B) tell us where
the *Pequod* is   (C) describe the hoisting of the casks
(D) show the depth of Ahab's obsession with Moby Dick

REMEMBERING DETAIL

2. When Starbuck did not obey him, Ahab
(A) threatened him with a musket   (B) told Flask to take
over   (C) went on deck   (D) listened to him

3. Starbuck wanted Ahab to
(A) order the ship to change course   (B) have the barrels
brought up and examined   (C) turn back to Nantucket
(D) have the leaking barrels thrown overboard

DRAWING CONCLUSIONS

4. You can tell from this chapter that
(A) Ahab wants to do right by the owners   (B) Ahab is
determined to take as much oil as possible   (C) Ahab does
not care what happens to his ship or crew as long as he gets
Moby Dick   (D) Ahab is afraid of the owners

USING YOUR REASON

5. When Ahab said "And I was not speaking or thinking of that at all. Begone! Let it leak!" he meant
   (A) all I care about is Moby Dick   (B) I don't want to lose any oil   (C) the weather is much too stormy to bring the casks on deck   (D) I don't believe we're going to lose enough oil to worry about

6. Starbuck wanted to up Burtons because he
   (A) wanted to save the oil for which the ship was making its voyage   (B) did not like the mess the leaking oil was making   (C) wanted to annoy Ahab   (D) wanted to give the crew something to do

IDENTIFYING THE MOOD

7. How must Starbuck have felt when Ahab threatened him with the loaded musket?
   (A) Annoyed   (B) Terrified   (C) Puzzled   (D) Amused

THINKING IT OVER

1. Why was Ahab so against Starbuck's suggestion that they up Burtons? Why do you think Ahab finally gave in?

2. Why do you think that Ahab eventually followed Starbuck's suggestion? Explain your answer.

CHAPTER 28

REMEMBERING DETAIL

1. Queequeg requested that
   (A) no one should come to visit him   (B) his coffin be kept out of his sight   (C) water and biscuits be put in the coffin   (D) Yojo be given to Ishmael

2. After he got better, Queequeg used his coffin as a
   (A) bed   (B) sea chest   (C) lifebuoy   (D) bench

DRAWING CONCLUSIONS

3. You can tell from this chapter that Ishmael thinks that
   (A) Queequeg does not work hard enough   (B) whaling men have easy lives   (C) he works harder than anyone   (D) captains do not work very hard

USING YOUR REASON

4. When Queequeg talked about "certain little canoes of dark wood" he meant

(A) coffins   (B) the canoes of his native island
(C) carved boxes   (D) sea chests
5. Queequeg became sick because
(A) being a harpooneer was too hard for him   (B) he worked in the bottom of the ship when the casks were being brought up   (C) he was not getting enough to eat   (D) he was homesick

CHAPTER 29

FINDING THE MAIN IDEA
1. This chapter is mainly about
(A) the blacksmith's family   (B) the special harpoon that Perth made for Ahab   (C) Ahab's knowledge of blacksmithing   (D) the blacksmith's shop

USING YOUR REASON
2. Ahab wanted the harpoon to be tempered with blood because he
(A) wanted the harpooneers to be bound to him in his fight
(B) thought it would temper the steel better than water
(C) believed it would insure the killing of Moby Dick
(D) wanted to follow an old custom of the harpooneers

IDENTIFYING THE MOOD
3. Which of the following best describes how Perth felt about the harpoon he was making?
(A) Proud   (B) Indifferent   (C) Pleased   (D) Uneasy

THINKING IT OVER
1. Why did Ahab take so much trouble over the harpoon that Perth was making for him?

CHAPTER 30

FINDING THE MAIN IDEA
1. In this chapter the author is mostly interested in
(A) showing that Ahab has no sense of humor
(B) describing the killing of four whales   (C) describing the luck of the *Bachelor*   (D) contrasting the *Bachelor*'s happy crew and the *Pequod*'s uneasy crew

REMEMBERING DETAIL

2. The *Bachelor*'s voyage had been
   (A) successful   (B) short   (C) dangerous   (D) boring
3. The try-works were a furnace used for
   (A) heating the ship   (B) cooking the oil from whale blubber   (C) cooking the crew's meals   (D) driving the engine in the ship

IDENTIFYING THE MOOD

4. When the crew of the *Pequod* saw the *Bachelor* on its way home, they were
   (A) angry   (B) glad   (C) pleased   (D) envious

THINKING IT OVER

1. Describe the contrast between the crews of the *Bachelor* and the *Pequod*. How would you have felt if you had been on the *Pequod* and had seen the other ship on its way home?
2. Does it seem to you that whalers sometimes have a casual attitude toward death? Explain.

CHAPTER 31

FINDING THE MAIN IDEA

1. In this chapter the author is mainly interested in
   (A) showing that nothing will turn Ahab from his purpose
   (B) describing a storm at sea   (C) telling about the corposants   (D) telling how a ship is equipped to deal with lightning

REMEMBERING DETAIL

2. One of the first things that happened in the storm was that
   (A) a man was swept overboard   (B) one of the ship's boats was lost   (C) the sea stove in the bottom of Ahab's boat   (D) Fedallah was injured by a falling mast
3. When it looked as though the sailors would no longer obey him, what did Ahab do?
   (A) Ran to his cabin   (B) Told Starbuck to go below decks
   (C) Threatened to kill the first sailor who changed the sails
   (D) Beat one of the sailors with his harpoon

USING YOUR REASON

4. Starbuck would like to have

(A) kept the lightning rods on board   (B) sung along with Stubb   (C) turned the ship around to take advantage of the wind and gone home   (D) sailed on into the storm

5. When the author said the *Pequod* "was torn of her canvas" he meant

(A) the sails were torn to shreds by the wind   (B) the sails had to be taken down because of the wind   (C) the sails were put up so the ship would sail better   (D) the sails were untouched by the storm

IDENTIFYING THE MOOD

6. Stubb's feeling during the storm was one of

(A) enjoyment   (B) pleasure   (C) fear   (D) awe

7. At the end of this chapter many of Ahab's crew felt

(A) great respect for him   (B) even more frightened of him than before   (C) proud to be members of his crew   (D) puzzled by his behavior

THINKING IT OVER

1. Ahab saw the corposants as a sign of good luck while Starbuck saw them as an ill omen. Why do you think they regarded the corposants so differently? With whom would you agree? Why?

CHAPTER 32

FINDING THE MAIN IDEA

1. The main point of this chapter is to show how

(A) the compasses went wrong   (B) a man was lost overboard   (C) Starbuck was tempted to kill Ahab   (D) Queequeg's coffin was made into a lifebuoy

REMEMBERING DETAIL

2. The ship was sailing in the wrong direction because

(A) the steersman was half asleep   (B) the compasses were out of order   (C) the crew had decided to disobey Ahab   (D) Starbuck had ordered the steersman to sail west instead of east

3. The lost lifebuoy was replaced by

(A) a lifebuoy brought from the storeroom   (B) a lifebuoy from a different part of the ship   (C) Queequeg's coffin   (D) nothing

DRAWING CONCLUSIONS

4. You can tell from this chapter that
(A) Ahab is a poor seaman   (B) Starbuck does not like his
wife and son   (C) Queequeg is superstitious   (D) Starbuck
thinks he will not live to see his wife and child again

IDENTIFYING THE MOOD

5. Because of all the things that were happening, the crew was
becoming more and more
(A) excited   (B) fearful   (C) happy   (D) angry

READING FOR DEEPER MEANING

6. Starbuck did not give in to the temptation to kill Ahab
because
(A) he was a coward   (B) Ahab woke up before he could
do it   (C) he was too decent a man to kill another
(D) Flask came down to the cabin before he could do it

THINKING IT OVER

1. Why did Starbuck think about killing Ahab? Why did he not
do it? What would you have done in his place?
2. The author describes in this chapter how Queequeg's coffin is
to be turned into a lifebuoy. Do you think that this creates
any particular kind of mood? Explain.

CHAPTER 33

FINDING THE MAIN IDEA

1. This chapter shows us how
(A) dangerous whaling can be   (B) Ahab buries all decent
feeling to chase the white whale   (C) Captain Gardiner lost
his son   (D) Ahab spent his time watching for Moby Dick

DRAWING CONCLUSIONS

2. Ahab ordered the *Pequod* to pull away from the funeral
service on the *Delight*
(A) out of politeness   (B) so his own crew would not think
of what might happen to them in the chase after Moby Dick
(C) because the *Delight*'s captain asked him to   (D) so the
Delight's crew would have room to throw the corpse overboard
3. Ahab would not stop to help Captain Gardiner search for his
son because he
(A) knew that the owners of the *Pequod* would not approve

(B) did not want to waste any time   (C) thought the son must already be dead   (D) knew that his crew would not like it

IDENTIFYING THE MOOD

4. It is clear in this chapter that the crew is becoming more and more
(A) superstitious   (B) angry   (C) pleased   (D) bored

READING FOR DEEPER MEANING

5. Ahab entrusted his life to Starbuck because he knew that
(A) there was no one else he could trust   (B) Starbuck was the chief mate   (C) Starbuck, however much he disliked the way the voyage was going, was a decent man
(D) Starbuck felt the same way about Moby Dick as he did

THINKING IT OVER

1. Ahab said to Captain Gardiner, "God bless ye, man, and may I forgive myself, but I must go." What does this statement tell you about Ahab?

2. When Ahab made Starbuck his watchman, he was putting his life into Starbuck's hands. If you were in Starbuck's place, would you have taken advantage of this opportunity? Explain.

CHAPTER 34

FINDING THE MAIN IDEA

1. In this chapter, the author is mainly interested in telling us
(A) about Starbuck's sadness at not being with wife and child
(B) about Ahab's life as a whaler   (C) about Ahab's wife and child   (D) that Ahab is sorry about what he is doing but cannot overcome his obsession

REMEMBERING DETAIL

2. Every morning, Starbuck's wife Mary
(A) carries their son to the hill to look for the first signs of Starbuck's ship   (B) sits at the window waiting for Starbuck to come home   (C) goes down to the sea to watch for Starbuck   (D) writes a letter to Starbuck

DRAWING CONCLUSIONS

3. For a time, Starbuck thinks that Ahab will
(A) wreck the *Pequod*   (B) give up the chase
(C) commit suicide   (D) have him killed

4. Ahab tells Starbuck that he must stay on board the *Pequod* during the chase after Moby Dick because
(A) he does not trust Starbuck   (B) Starbuck has a wife and child, and this arouses Ahab's feelings of decency
(C) he thinks that Starbuck is a coward   (D) Starbuck is the best man to look after the *Pequod*

THINKING IT OVER

1. Ahab knows very well that his obsession with Moby Dick is both foolish and dangerous. Can you explain why he cannot give up the chase?

CHAPTER 35

FINDING THE MAIN IDEA

1. In this chapter the author is mostly interested in telling us about
(A) the first sighting of Moby Dick   (B) the first day's chase after Moby Dick   (C) what happened to Ahab's boat
(D) Moby Dick's huge size

REMEMBERING DETAIL

2. What happened to Ahab's boat in the chase after Moby Dick?
(A) It ran into the *Pequod*.   (B) Nothing.   (C) Moby Dick bit it in two.   (D) It lost its oars.

3. Ahab ordered Starbuck to have some of the sails taken down because
(A) he wanted to overtake Moby Dick during the night
(B) the sails were torn   (C) he did not want to sail over Moby Dick during the night   (D) it was good practice for the sailors

DRAWING CONCLUSIONS

4. You can tell from this chapter that Ahab is
(A) a very experienced whaler   (B) an inexperienced whaler   (C) a poor seaman   (D) a cowardly seaman

THINKING IT OVER

1. After reading this chapter, do you find any qualities to admire in Ahab? Explain.

2. If you had been in the first day's chase after Moby Dick, would you have wanted to go back for more? Explain.

CHAPTER 36

FINDING THE MAIN IDEA

1. In this chapter the author is mainly interested in
(A) telling about the death of Fedallah   (B) describing the second day's chase after Moby Dick   (C) describing the mood of the crew   (D) showing how brave and cunning Moby Dick is

REMEMBERING DETAIL

2. What happened to the boats of Stubb and Flask?
(A) Moby Dick dragged them under the sea.   (B) They crashed into each other.   (C) They lost their oars.
(D) Moby Dick threw them into the air.
3. What happened to Ahab?
(A) He broke his arm.   (B) He was knocked out.   (C) His ivory leg was snapped off.   (D) He was drowned.
4. Who was lost during the second day's chase?
(A) Queequeg   (B) Starbuck   (C) Dough-Boy
(D) Fedallah

IDENTIFYING THE MOOD

5. In the confrontation between Ahab and Starbuck it is clear that
(A) Ahab will die rather than give up the chase   (B) Ahab will kill Moby Dick   (C) the crew backs Starbuck
(D) Starbuck is surprised
6. On the second day of the chase, the crew's mood was
(A) somber   (B) fearful   (C) enthusiastic   (D) angry

THINKING IT OVER

1. Why is it that the crew is suddenly no longer fearful?
2. What does the author mean when he says that "They were one man, not thirty"?

CHAPTER 37

FINDING THE MAIN IDEA

1. The main purpose of this chapter is to show
(A) how the confrontation between Ahab and Moby Dick ends   (B) what had happened to Fedallah   (C) how the sharks acted during the third day's chase   (D) how

Starbuck felt when he saw Ahab go after Moby Dick again

USING YOUR REASON

2. When Ahab said "I will harpoon the first man that offers to jump from the boat I stand in" he meant
(A) I want someone to leave this boat   (B) I want all of you to leave this boat   (C) I will kill anyone who tries to run away from the chase now   (D) I do not want anyone unwilling in this boat

3. Ahab sent the other boats back to the ship because he
(A) did not like the way the crews were fighting Moby Dick
(B) knew they were damaged   (C) wanted the glory of killing Moby Dick to himself   (D) did not want any of the other crews to die

DRAWING CONCLUSIONS

4. You can tell from Ahab's remarks to Starbuck as he leaves the ship for the third day's chase that he
(A) knows he will not be coming back   (B) is getting tired of the chase   (C) wants Starbuck to persuade him not to go
(D) expects to kill Moby Dick on that day

5. What happened to the *Pequod?*
(A) It got away safely.   (B) Nothing.   (C) It lost some of its sails.   (D) Moby Dick sank it.

IDENTIFYING THE MOOD

6. Which of the following best describes Ahab's emotions as he prepares to die?
(A) Hatred   (B) Fear   (C) Sorrow   (D) Anger

THINKING IT OVER

1. The author ends this chapter with the sentence "And the great sea rolled on as it rolled five thousand years ago." What do you think he meant by that? Explain your answer.

2. Do you think that Starbuck felt only hatred for Ahab? Do you think he had any other feelings about Ahab? Explain.

CHAPTER 38

THINKING IT OVER

1. What does the author mean when he says, "It was the *Rachel,* who, still hunting her missing children, had found only me, another orphan"?